The Author

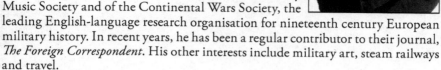

Robert Mantle has been studying military history and military music for most of his life, but his interest in the 1866 campaign goes back forty years, when he first read Gordon Craig's classic *The Battle of Königgrätz*. Since then he has built up a library of books and articles on the subject and was able to visit the battlefields themselves in 2001.

He is a member of the International Military Music Society and of the Continental Wars Society, the leading English-language research organisation for nineteenth century European military history. In recent years, he has been a regular contributor to their journal, *The Foreign Correspondent*. His other interests include military art, steam railways and travel.

After thirty-five years as a local government officer, he is now retired and lives in South East London. He is married to Susie, who tolerates an increasing number of books and CDs in their house.

MILITARY MUSIC
IN THE CAMPAIGN
OF 1866

by

Robert Mantle

Helion & Company Ltd

Helion & Company Limited
26 Willow Road
Solihull
West Midlands B91 1UE
England
Tel. 0121 705 3393
Fax 0121 711 4075
Email: info@ helion.co.uk
Website: www.helion.co.uk

Published by Helion & Company 2009

Designed and typeset by Farr out Publications, Wokingham, Berkshire
Printed by Cpod, Trowbridge, Wiltshire

Text © Robert Mantle 2007

The illustrations are drawn from the collections of the author and Duncan Rogers.

ISBN 978-1-906033-50-7

British Library Cataloguing-in-Publication Data. A catalogue record for this book
is available from the British Library.

For details of other military history titles published by Helion & Company
Limited contact the above address, or visit our website: www.helion.co.uk.

We always welcome receiving book proposals from prospective authors.

Contents

Introduction

The brief, dramatic conflict that erupted in Central Europe in Summer 1866 saw a modern army pitted against one that had hardly changed since the Napoleonic period. It was Europe's first real glimpse of the Prussian staff system, the true reason for their victory. Military bands played a relatively minor role, but they were an essential part of contemporary military life and popular culture. In fact, the period 1840–1870 is often seen as a golden age for military music in Austria and Prussia. The war of 1866 was one of the last in which bands accompanied their units into action – often with grim consequences.

This study attempts to explain the background to the music played in the campaign and to give an idea of the bands' organisation and the personalities who influenced it. Much of the material has never been translated and I hope it will be helpful to the English-speaking reader.

I would like to dedicate this book to the memory of the military musicians of both sides who served alongside their comrades on the battlefields of Bohemia.

Robert Mantle

Chapter 1

Prussia: The Wieprecht Era

The development of military music

By 1800, Prussian infantry bands were evolving from small ensembles of wind players (*Harmoniemusik*) and combining with the "Turkish" or "Janissary" music of the percussion players and the drums and fifes of the company musicians. The light infantry, (Fusiliers, *Jäger* and *Schützen*) relied on their horn players, while the cavalry massed their trumpeters on parade.

The catastrophe of 1806–1807 swept away not only the majority of Prussia's regiments, but also much of their musical repertoire. The new Prussian army had a limited budget and music was a low priority: nevertheless, by 1812 the Foot Guards had a band twenty four strong, while the Line regiments averaged nine to ten musicians. Rifle battalions had eight horn players under a *Stabshornist*, while in the cavalry, the Trumpet Major controlled twelve trumpeters and, in some regiments, a kettledrummer.

After Napoleon's defeat and exile, there were moves to establish a unified system of military music. The model was the Russian army, whose bands and choral singing had impressed King Friedrich Wilhelm III. Since 1809, the bands of the Russian Guards had been supervised by their Inspector of Music, Anton Dörfeldt (1781–1829), a tireless composer and arranger who had compiled a collection of slow and quick marches, which would form the basis of the official Prussian collection described below. The next step came on July 18th, 1819, when Georg Abraham Schneider was appointed Inspector of Music to the Guard and Grenadier Corps.

Schneider (1770–1839) was a talented horn player and composer whose remit involved examining band masters and musicians, producing scores and expanding the Army's repertoire. By the time he retired, a whole generation of outstanding bandmasters had grown up: possibly the best was August-Heinrich Neithardt, who took over the 33-strong band of the Kaiser Franz Grenadier Regiment in 1822. The "Franzers", like the other units of the Berlin garrison, regularly gave concerts in the Lustgarten opposite the Royal Palace, during the daily ceremony of Changing the Guard and one day in May 1824, a trombonist from the Royal Opera took a break from rehearsals and followed the sound of music to where Neithardt and his men were performing the overture to Mozart's *The Marriage of Figaro*. Later, the trombonist wrote that their performance was a revelation; their playing reduced him to tears of delight and "I felt myself called in this direction and saw at a glance that I would achieve something in this field!" It was the beginning of Wilhelm Wieprecht's career in military music.

Wieprecht's first efforts involved the cavalry and the new valved brass instruments. He developed a working relationship with the Guard Dragoons: *Six Marches for Cavalry Band* appeared in 1825 and the Dragoons' C.O, Colonel von

9

Prussia: the band of the 13th Infantry Regiment, c.1855. The helmet was replaced by a lower model in 1860. Note the fringes on the bandmaster's 'swallow's nests'.

Barner paid 400 Thalers from his own pocket for new instruments. In the next few years, Wieprecht travelled to various garrisons to train their musicians and built up a network of contacts, including members of the Royal Family. This hard work paid off on February 2nd, 1838, when he succeeded Schneider as Inspector of Music for the Guard Corps and, by implication, the whole Prussian Army. This appointment was resented in some quarters; no one doubted Wieprecht's talents, but he was a civilian and a very unmilitary looking one at that, as this contemporary description of him at a rehearsal shows:

> Wieprecht conducted with passion. A small man, he stood on a stool and explained, with gestures, what the piece involved. He hopped, waved his arms and turned from side to side until the sweat stood out on his brow, his neckcloth came undone and he had to mop himself down with a large silk handkerchief.

Many felt that a serving soldier would have been a better choice and the document appointing Wieprecht (drawn up for Prince Wilhelm, the future king and emperor) makes it clear that he would be kept under close scrutiny. Throughout his career, he would remain an official, addressed as "Herr Wieprecht": the frock coat he wore on duty had no epaulettes or badges of rank and he was not entitled to a salute. If some long-serving bandmasters gave Wieprecht a chilly reception, the public flocked to his concerts at Renz's Circus and the Victoria Theatre. In 1846, Friedrich Sass wrote that "If Prussia's military bandsmen are the best in Europe, we should not forget _____ the service that Herr Wieprecht has rendered in training them."

Wieprecht's speciality was the "monster concert", with hundreds of musicians. In 1844, he conducted the massed bands of the Federal X Corps – 820 musicians and 300 drummers from Hanover, Brunswick, Mecklenburg, Oldenburg and the Hanseatic cities – and the following year, 560 Prussian bandsmen and 136 drummers performed before Queen Victoria at Schloss Bruhl, near Cologne. There were no printed band parts until 1914 and these concerts must have involved copying on a vast scale. One of Wieprecht's campaigns was for a standardised system of scoring, so that, in his own words "he could travel anywhere with one score" and in 1860, the Prussian War Ministry decreed that only Wieprecht's arrangements were to be used in future.

Meanwhile, the development of valved instruments was changing the size and character of bands. The keyed bugle, or "Kenthorn" had been invented around 1810 and we have seen how Wieprecht used the new instruments in his first experiments. In 1835, Johann Gottfried Moritz invented the tuba and the problem of the "bassline" was solved. The earlier stopgaps – serpents, "basshorns" and ophicleides – began to disappear and bands acquired the sound we recognise today, dominated by brass instruments.

With his background in classical music, it was natural for Wieprecht to see bands as "military orchestras" and his work was praised by the leading composers of his day, such as Meyerbeer and Liszt. In a letter of July 18th, 1855, Liszt addresses Wieprecht as "Dear friend", congratulates him on his arrangements of his work and looks forward to his arrangement of the symphonic poem *Tasso*,

Wilhelm Wieprecht (1802-1872), the dominant
personality in Prussian military music during this period.

giving him a free hand to adapt the score. Perhaps the best-known comments are in Hector Berlioz's memoirs. Visiting Berlin 1843, he praised Wieprecht's "regiments of musicians" and was deeply moved when, at a concert before Prince and Princess Wilhelm, he heard an arrangement of his own *Francs-Juges* overture, claiming that no French orchestra could have played it as well as the Prussian Guards did!

In all these years of composing, arranging, conducting and training, Wieprecht met with only one defeat. For some reason, he disliked the distinctive all-brass ensembles of the *Jäger* and *Schützen* battalions and wished to introduce woodwind to them: he met his match in Johann Gottfried Rode, the redoubtable bandmaster of the Guard Jäger Battalion and the struggle only ended with Rode's death in 1857. The Jäger retained their distinctive sound until the Second World War.

On February 2nd, 1863, the massed bands of the Berlin garrison assembled outside Wieprecht's apartment at 34, Unter den Linden and played a serenade to celebrate his Silver Jubilee as Inspector of Army Music. The former outsider was now the leading figure in Prussian military music, though his greatest triumph was still to come.

Prussian bands: three distinctive styles

In nineteenth-century Prussia (and the other German states) the principal branches of the army each had their distinctive musical style, which they would retain until

1945. Each infantry battalion had a corps of drums and fifes (*spielleute*) which could be combined on parade with the Drum Major of the 1st Battalion acting as the *Regimentstambour*. These were "company musicians", distinct from the band. The familiar shallow side drum (*flachtrommel*) was introduced in 1854 and soon supplanted the cylindrical model. Both types had brass shells with the upper and lower rims painted with alternative red and white triangles; the drum was attached to the waistbelt by a brass clip with a badge shaped like an eagle. Fifes were carried in a cylindrical leather case on a shoulder belt; the cases were red leather until 1854, then black with brass fittings. The fifers also carried a bugle, the shape of which was closer to a cavalry trumpet than the British style. When the drums paraded with the band, they were often accompanied by a *Schellenbaum*, adapted from the "jingling Johnny" carried by the Turkish janissaries and which has always reminded this author of a mobile totem pole. It had no musical role and was always carried by the tallest man in the regiment.

The band itself, usually referred to as a *Musikkorps*, comprised *hoboisten* – professional musicians – and *hilfshoboisten* – soldiers from the ranks, who had been taught to play an instrument and who could, in theory, be returned to their companies in wartime. By 1860, the average band had a strength of 35 to 40 men, composed as follows:

1 Piccolo 2 Flutes 2 Oboes 8 Clarinets
2 Bassoons 1 Contrabassoon 4 Trumpets 5 Horns
1 Bombardon 3 Trombones 1 "Bass Horn"
1 Side Drum 1 Bass Drum 1 Pair Cymbals 1 Triangle

Some of these instruments would soon be obsolete; the bombardon (which was carried around the musician's body like a sousaphone) and the bass horn were replaced by tubas and the triangle was replaced after 1865 by the glockenspiel.

Bands rarely exceeded 40 men, even after 1860, when strengths were established at 42. Even the Guards regiments kept at this level and Wieprecht had to combine two bands for the Paris Exhibition in 1867. An exception was the band of the 34th Fusiliers, garrisoned in the Federal fortress of Rastatt and who gave regular concerts in the fashionable spa of Baden-Baden: their bandmaster, Albert Parlow, managed to raise the strength of his band to 62!

The band was led by a *Stabshoboist*, a trained bandsman who ranked as a senior NCO. (When the civilian Friedrich Wilhelm Voigt was appointed as *Stabshoboist* of the 1st Foot Guards in 1857, he had to be enlisted and given a (very) basic recruit's course.) Meritorious service could earn promotion to "Royal Music Director" (*Koniglich Musikdirektor*) but never to commissioned rank. King Friedrich Wilhelm IV's inclusion of *Stabshoboist* Wilhelm Christoph in his entourage for the royal visit to Vienna in 1853 was regarded as a rare honour.

This style of instrumentation was also used by the Field Artillery until they became a "mounted corps" in 1860 and by the "Foot" (Heavy) Artillery.

The musicians of the Rifle Battalions (*Jäger* and *Schützen*) were known as *Waldhornisten*, reflecting their origins as huntsmen and gamekeepers. Despite Wieprecht's efforts, they never used woodwind or percussion. A typical band of 1857 consisted of:

Prussia: Kettledrummer of the Garde du
Corps, parade dress, by Herbert Knötel.

Prussia: Trumpeter, 1st Cuirassiers,
by Herbert Knötel.

Prussia: Trumpeter, 12th
Hussars, by Herbert Knötel.

Prussia: Trumpeter, 9th Lancers
(full dress), by Herbert Knötel.

1 E flat Cornet 2 Soprano Cornets 1 *"Alt-Kornett"* 3 Trumpets
6 Horns 2 Tenor Horns 1 *"Bariton"*
1 Tenor Trombone 1 Bass Trombone 1 Bass Tuba

The *Alt-Kornett* may have been a variant of the keyed bugle and the *Bariton* was an early version of the euphonium. The ensemble was led by a *Stabswaldhornist* whose rank and career prospects were the same as for his colleague in the infantry. This style of instrumentation was also used by Engineer units (*Pioniere*). Finally, we should note that Prussian riflemen never used the accelerated marching pace of the British, French and Italian light infantry.

Cavalry bands had developed far more slowly, partly because of the late development of valved instruments. In addition, it was the custom, in the first half of the nineteenth century, to deploy cavalry regiments by squadrons, separated by over twenty kilometres of unmetalled road. The trumpeters, three to a squadron, formed the basis and were commanded by a Trumpet Major (*Stabstrompeter*). Some regiments also had kettledrums, often a war trophy.

Wieprecht's original scheme for the Guard Dragoons consisted of:
6 Trumpets 2 *"Klapperhorns"* (another variant of the keyed bugle)
2 Tenor Horns 1 "Tenor-Bass-Horn" 2 Bass Trombones

By the 1840s, cavalry bands were all-brass ensembles of between 15 and 20 men; the regulations of 1856 set their establishment as a Trumpet Major, three trumpeters per squadron and nine *Hilfstrompeter*. The *"klapperhorns"* and "tenor-bass-horns" had been replaced by now by trombones and bombardons.

Cavalry trumpets were brass, 40cm long for Guards regiments and 42cm for the Line. Their cords and tassels were either yellow or white (depending on the colour of the regiment's buttons and lace) with a line of the regimental facing colour. When the Field Artillery became a "mounted corps" in 1860, they adopted Trompeterkorps like the cavalry.

Musicians' Dress Distinctions

The distinguishing mark of a Prussian musician was the "swallow's nest" (*schwalbennest*), a semicircular piece of cloth attached to the top of each sleeve. They were always in the same colour as the tunic's collar and had eight vertical bars of lace, with a broad band of lace along the lower edge. Infantry *spielleute* wore white lace, but infantry and *Jäger* bandsmen wore gold or silver lace, depending on their unit's "button colour". *Hoboisten* ranked as NCOs and wore this lace on their collars and cuffs, as did *Hilfshoboisten*, who ranked as junior NCOs. From 1846, Guards musicians wore fringes on their "swallow's nests"; these were 5.5cm long for *spielleute*, 3cm long for bandsmen and 7cm for *Stabshoboisten*, *Stabswaldhornisten* and Drum Majors. Line Bandmasters and Drum Majors gained this distinction in the following year. Cavalry trumpeters ranked as NCOs but *Hilfstrompeter* ranked as troopers.

The Foot Guards, Dragoons and some Line infantry regiments wore helmet plumes on parade: these were red for musicians. *Jäger* wore red drooping plumes in their shakos; Lancers and Hussars wore identical plumes in their headdress. Cuirassier trumpeters wore red plumes on parade and did not wear the cuirass.

The Army March Collection

February 10th, 1817

To help regiments choose good military music, I have had a selection of good marches compiled and each regiment will be given a copy of this collection. In order to improve the troops' repertoire, it is My wish that only music from this collection should be played in future at all ceremonials, parades and reviews, especially those where I am present.

Friedrich Wilhelm

This decree marks the beginning of the Prussian Army March Collection (*Armeemarsch-Sammlung*) which would continue until 1929. The original collection, based on Anton Dörfeldt's Russian collection, was in two volumes, each containing thirty-six pieces, with Volume I containing slow marches and Volume II quick ones, all scored for the contemporary infantry band. The majority were of Russian origin, but included some pre-1806 Prussian marches. A third volume, containing marches for cavalry band was begun in 1824. Each march was assigned a number, prefixed with the letters AM, with the volume number in Roman numerals and the individual march's number in Arabic. Thus the slow march *Herzog von Braunschweig* was AM I, 9, the quick march of the Russian Semeonovski Guards was AM II, 62 and the *Kavalleriemarsch* composed by Wieprecht for the Guard Dragoons was AM III, 21.

Prussia: *Schellenbaumträger*, Emperor Alexander Guard Grenadier Regiment, full dress, by Herbert Knötel.

Georg Goldschmidt (1823-1903). Trained by Gottfried Piefke, he led the band of the 7th (King's) Grenadiers from 1858 to 1897.

Prussia: Drummer, Emperor Francis Grenadier Regiment, 1858, by Ludwig
Burger. By 1866, the helmet had been replaced by a lower model.

As the collection evolved over the following decades, slow marches fell out of favour: only thirteen were added to Volume I in its first ten years and four more in the next eleven. Finally, in 1841, six eighteenth century Prussian marches were added, after which the volume remained dormant until 1895. (The slow march was replaced by the *Präsentiermarsch* or General Salute). Volume II, however, went from strength to strength; the 50th march was added in 1820, the 100th in 1834 and the 150th in 1853. By 1866, the volume contained 193 marches. Volume III progressed more slowly; reaching AM III, 63 in 1865.

The marches in the collection are from various sources; the close family links between the Hohenzollerns and the Romanovs resulted in many Russian marches being added, while royal visits to Austrian territories or the Italian states produced another group of musical "souvenirs". Many are based on themes from operas or ballets, while others were added for political reasons – or simply because a member of the royal family liked them. (In 1863, Crown Princess Victoria asked for two of her favourite "English" melodies to be arranged as a march. Her father-in-law, King Wilhelm ordered that it become an Army March, but it is unlikely that AM II 187 *Marsch über das Lied* 'The Bluebells of Scotland' *und* 'The Rifle Brigade Marsch'" was ever played unless the Princess requested it.) But the core was formed of compositions or arrangements by Prussian bandmasters; Neithardt, for example had fourteen items in the collection by the time he retired.

Selection for the collection was no guarantee of a permanent place in the repertoire: many marches fell out of favour as years went by, or were never played. The majority of the material added before 1850 suffered this fate and remained unheard until it was recorded for a series of LPs in the 1980s. The prize marches from Bote & Bock's competitions in the 1850s (see below) also consigned many good contemporary marches to obscurity.

Although bands were confined to material from the collection when on parade, they had a completely free choice of marches when on the march, or when giving a concert. For example, Wieprecht's march *Links-Rechts* ("Left, Right!") was performed during the serenade outside his apartment at 34, Unter den Linden, but could not be played at the Guard Changing ceremony at the palace, a few hundred yards away!

The Army March Collection, like any collection, is of uneven quality. It contains most of the classic Prussian marches and many more that deserve at least a second hearing.

Berlin's Golden Era

By the mid 1850s, Wilhelm Wieprecht was the dominant figure in Prussian military music, but there were several other outstanding personalities in the field. The best known were in the Berlin garrison, but there were many others in the provinces: Emil Winter in Danzig, Georg Faust in the Federal fortress of Luxembourg, Georg Goldschmidt in Liegntzand, above all, Gottfried Piefke in Frankfurt an der Oder.

The surviving portraits of Piefke show him in middle age: a stocky man with a receding hairline, sidewhiskers and a chest full of decorations. Only the bristling eyebrows give a hint of the self assured young man of thirty years before who had made enemies and caused a scandal. His appointment as *Stabshoboist*

Kapellmeister Piefke vom Leibregiment.
Photographed after his return to
Frankfurt-an-der-Oder.

of the 8th Infantry Regiment in 1843 seems to have channelled all his energies into his music; he mastered every instrument in his band, which soon became the equivalent of a symphony orchestra. Piefke's arrangements of Weber, Mozart, Mendelssohn and Beethoven were the closest many of his audience would come to the original score and in 1858, Hans von Bülow, one of the leading conductors of the day, wrote an article praising his arrangement of Beethoven's Seventh Symphony. His favourite composer was Richard Wagner and his arrangement of the overtures to *Tannhauser* and *Lohengrin* won wide acclaim.

In July 1852, the Headquarters and I Battalion of the 8th Regiment, with their band, moved to Berlin, where they remained until 1860. (They were the only Line regiment in the garrison and the Berliners, seeing the woven figure 8 on their shoulder straps, dubbed them *"Die Brezelgarde* – 'The Pretzel Guards'".) Now Piefke was performing alongside some of the country's best musicians: the 2nd Foot Guards under Gottfried Christian Meinberg, the Emperor Alexander Grenadiers under Carl Liebig, the Emperor Franz Grenadiers under Wilhelm Christoph, the Guard Schützen Battalion under Johann Carl Neumann and the 2nd Guard Lancers under Albert Lorenz. All these bands were a familiar sight at the daily Guard Mounting ceremony, which always included a concert. In addition to this ceremony and the parades on Tempelhof Field, the bands gave regular lunchtime and evening recitals. An advertisement in the *Neuer Berliner Musikzeitung* of July 7th, 1858 gives details of two concerts to take place the following day, at the *Hofjäger* beer garden and the Odeum theatre, to raise money for invalid bandsmen and for bandsmen's widows and orphans. The Odeum concert featured the bands of the Alexander Grenadiers, the 8th Infantry and the Guard Heavy Artillery, the Guard Schützen's brass ensemble and the trumpet corps of the 2nd Guard Lancers and the Guard Horse Artillery. At the *Hofjäger*, where you could hear the 2nd Foot Guards, the Guard Reserve Regiment (later

Donnerstag, den 8. Juli:

GROSSES

RÉUNION - CONCERT

im

ODEUM und HOFJÆGER,

zum Besten der

Hof-Musikhändler Bock'schen Spezial-Stiftung

zur Unterstützung invalider Militair-Musiker und Spielleute, wie deren Wittwen und Waisen

veranstaltet von

sämmtlichen Infanterie- und Cavallerie-Musik-Chören

der Berliner Garnison.

ODEUM.

Die Musik-Chöre des Kaiser-Alexander-Grenadier-, Garde-Fuss-Artillerie-, 8ten Leib-Infanterie-, Garde-Ulanen-, reitenden Garde-Artillerie-Regiments und des Garde-Schützen-Bataillons.

ERSTER THEIL.

*Victoria-Marsch	Wleprecht.
Ouvertüre zur Cantate „Die vier Menschenalter"	Lachner.
*Serenade	Mendelssohn.
Man lebt nur einmal, Walzer	Strauss.
*Preis-Marsch (der 25. Mai 1858)	Albert Lorenz.
Mazurka aus dem Ballet „Morgano"	Hertel.

ZWEITER THEIL.

*Ouvertüre zur Oper „Die Zigeunerin"	Balfe.
Ave Maria aus der Oper „Indra"	F. v. Flotow.
*Galopp aus dem Ballet „Morgano"	Hertel.
Introduction aus der Oper „Die Lombarden"	Verdi.
*Humoristische Rundschau, Fantasie	Strauss.
Armee-Marsch (No. 170)	Löhrcke.

DRITTER THEIL.

*Festmarsch aus dem Fest „Die weisse Rose"	Graf v. Redern.
Chor aus der Oper „Die Nibelungen"	Dorn.
*Sanssouci-Polka	Faust.
Preis-Marsch (1857)	Lübbert.

Zapfenstreich.

HOFJÆGER.

Die Musik-Chöre des 2. Garde-, Garde-Reserve-, Kaiser Franz-, Garde-Kürassier-, Garde-Dragoner-Regiments und ein Tambour-Chor.

ERSTER THEIL.

Zwei Preis-Märsche pro 1858	a) Buchholz.	b) Neumann.
Ouvertüre zur Oper „Don Juan"	Mozart.	
*Finale aus der Oper „Die Hugenotten"	Meyerbeer.	
Schallwellen, Walzer	Joh. Strauss.	
**Marsch und Chor aus der Oper „Tannhäuser"	Wagner.	

ZWEITER THEIL.

Ouvertüre zu „Egmont"	L. v. Beethoven.
*Aric aus der Oper „Der Troubadour"	Verdi.
Chor und Tanz aus der Oper „Macbeth"	Taubert.
*Polka-Mazurka aus dem Ballet „Morgano"	Hertel.
**Fackeltanz zur Vermählungsfeier S. Kgl. Hoh. des Prinzen Friedrich Wilhelm von Preussen	Meyerbeer.
**Quadrille à cheval	Graf v. Redern.

DRITTER THEIL.

**Ouvertüre zur Oper „Ein Feldlager in Schlesien	Meyerbeer.
*Duett aus der Oper „Maritana"	Wallace.
Introduction und Chor aus der Oper „Lohengrin"	Wagner.
*Ouvertüre zur Oper „Titus"	Mozart.
Frühlings-Fantasien, Walzer	Jos. Gung'l.
**Hochzeitsmarsch a. d. „Sommernachtstraum"	Mendelssohn.

Die mit einem * bezeichneten Piecen werden von den Cavallerie-Musik-Chören, und die mit ** bezeichneten von allen vereinigten Chören ausgeführt.

Der Anfang des Concerts ist 6 Uhr.

Billets à 5 Sgr., zu beiden Lokalen gültig, sind in der Königl. Hof-Musikhandlung des Herrn G. Bock, Jägerstrasse No. 42, Unter den Linden No. 27 und an der Kasse à 7½ Sgr. zu haben.

Sämmtlich angezeigte Musikalien zu beziehen durch Ed. **Bote & G. Bock** in Berlin und Posen.

Verlag von Ed. **Bote & G. Bock** (G. Bock, Königl. Hof-Musikhändler) in Berlin, Jägerstr. No. 42 und U. d. Linden No. 27.

Druck von C. F. Schmidt in Berlin, Unter den Linden No. 30.

Aus: Neue Berliner Musikzeitung vom 7. Juli 1858

An advertisment in the *Neuer Berliner Musikzeitung* of July 7th 1858, announcing two concerts for the following day.

the Guard Fusiliers), the "Franzers", the Guard Cuirassiers, the Guard Dragoons and a corps of drums, the concert began with the three infantry bands playing the two prizewinning marches from that year's Bote & Bock competition, followed by the overture to Mozart's *Don Giovanni*. Then the cavalry took over with an arrangement of the finale to Meyerbeer's *The Huguenots*. The infantry played

Strauss's waltz *Schallwellen* and finally the massed bands played the *Pilgrims' Chorus* from *Tannhauser*. This was only the first part of the concert: both concerts consisted of three parts and although both began at 6pm, one wonders when the audience finally went home! The concerts were organised by the publishing firm of Bote & Bock, who had already made a major contribution to Berlin's musical life with their prize competitions. The idea came from Gustav Bock (1813-1863) who organised the first competition in 1851. Entries had to be submitted under a pseudonym, with the composer's true identity in a sealed envelope; the judging was held at the Royal Theatre on the Gendarmenmarkt on February 12th, 1852 and was a success, with five of the twelve finalists winning prizes. The competition was limited to bandmasters, but from 1852 onwards, any Prussian soldier could take part.

Over the next eight years, the competition became a popular social occasion. Thirty-five prizes were awarded: the most successful entrant was Albert Lorenz with seven prizes, followed by Emil Winter with four and Carl Neumann, Heinrich Saro and Friedrich Zikoff with two each. Fifteen marches – three by Lorenz, two by Winter and both of Saro's – became Army Marches and many, such as Faust's *Defiliermarsch* or Lübbert's *Helenenmarsch* are still played today.

For the 1858 competition, two sergeant musicians from the Kaiser Alexander Grenadier Regiment were encouraged by their bandmaster, Carl Liebig, to submit marches. That year, Eduard Bucholz gained Second Prize with *Soldatenklänge* ("Soldier's Melody") and Emil Neumann won First Prize with his *Viktoria-Marsch*. (These were the two marches that opened the Hofjaeger concert). Both became Army Marches in 1860.

A competition was planned for 1862, but never occurred as Gustav Bock had fallen terminally ill. He had given much pleasure to the public and helped produce some classic marches: military music owes much to him.

The expansion of the Army in 1860–1861 had relatively little effect on the Berlin garrison as the four new Guards regiments were stationed in the provinces, but the 8th Infantry – now a Grenadier Regiment – was reunited in Frankfurt an der Oder. One of the bandsmen – Piefke's brother Rudolf – became Bandmaster of the newly-formed 48th Infantry in Küstrin.

A sign of the times came on January 18th, 1861, when the colours and standards of the new regiments were paraded on Unter den Linden, carried by the *Leibkompagnie* of the 1st Foot Guards (the equivalent of the Queen's Company Grenadier Guards), dressed in greatcoats and wearing their ceremonial "Russian" mitre caps. They were accompanied by their regimental band and corps of drums, also in greatcoats, but wearing their helmets with red horsehair plumes. With the band playing Beethoven's *Marsch des Yorck 'schen Korps*, the parade marched down the avenue to the statue of Frederick the Great, where the colours were consecrated. Cheering crowds lined the route and the scene inspired Gustav Loewenthal, the newly-appointed bandmaster of the 3rd (Queen Elisabeth's) Guard Grenadiers to compose his *Fahnenweihemarsch* ("Blessing the Colours"), which became an Army March almost immediately. It remained popular until 1934, when the then Inspector of Army Music, Hermann Schmidt, struck it from the collection in the erroneous belief that Loewenthal was Jewish.

In the next decade, Berlin would become the capital of a united Germany and develop into a great industrial city, where military ceremonial would be part of daily life. The Berlin of the 1850s was a smaller, more attractive place, where the art of military music reached one of its high points.

Chapter 2

Austria: The Leonhardt Era

"Musical Missionaries"

I n 1857, the Viennese music critic Eduard Hanslick wrote that:

> The headquarters of a regiment is often located in places where the inhabitants have never heard an orchestra – or such a full and clear musical sound – before. Small wonder that it leaves such an impression -- The bandsman are true musical missionaries, bringing the joyful gospel of art into previously silent lands.

Unlike Prussia, Austria was a multinational, multilingual empire, whose cities included Krakow, Zagreb and Venice.Military bands were an integral part of its culture and a band concert was a regular feature of garrison life. As Hanslick points out, it was often the first chance for a community to hear the great classical works in a form that approached the composer's intentions. It was also a symbol of Habsburg authority. In Italy, people who paid too much attention to an "Austrian" concert might be suspected of disloyalty by the nationalists and John Ruskin, in *The Stones of Venice*, describes a band playing on St Mark's Square, with the Italians glowering as their music drowned out the *Miserere* being sung in the cathedral.

As in Prussia, there were three types of band – infantry, *Jäger* and cavalry – and all followed the same style. They also maintained the distinction between professional musicians (*Hoboisten* or *Hautboisten*) and soldiers serving with the band (*Bandisten*). The whole ensemble was usually referred to as a *Musikbanda*, or simply as a *Banda*. In charge was a *Kapellmeister* and this individual came in two forms. "Obliged" (*Obligater*) bandmasters were long-serving musicians appointed by their commanding officer and who ranked (unofficially) as NCOs, but these worthy men were normally found in regiments stationed in the more remote corners of the empire. Far more common was the *Unobligater*, a civilian musician engaged by contract. In 1854, for example, the newly formed 8th Dragoons placed an advertisement in the newspaper *Der Oesterreichische Soldatenfreund*, offering a prospective *Kapellmeister* 60 florins a month, with free quarters and uniform. The successful candidate would be on a temporary contract until he had satisfied the regiment as to his abilities, when he would be formally engaged and receive 100 gulden. Unfortunately, we do not know the outcome – but as the 8th Dragoons were disbanded in1860, it would not have been a long engagement. Nevertheless, many well-known musicians took up similar appointments: the brothers Josef and Philipp Fahrbach both signed contracts in 1841. Josef served with the 45th (Baron Meyer) Infantry until 1844, when he transferred to the 44th (Archduke Albrecht) Regiment, remaining with them until he resigned in 1848. Meanwhile, his younger brother had served five years with the 4th (Hoch-und-

Deutschmeister) Regiment. After several successful years leading an orchestra in Vienna, Philipp rejoined the Army in 1856 and served with the 14th (Grand Duke of Hesse) Regiment until 1865, seeing action in two campaigns. Similarly, Josef Gung'l, who had previously served with the 4th, then the 5th Artillery between 1828 and 1843, took up the baton again with the 23rd (Baron Airoldi) Regiment between 1856 and 1864.

The *Kapellmeister*'s duties included training musicians, supervising their performance and maintaining a repertoire. (The candidate for the 8th Dragoons was also expected to recruit bandsmen and obtain instruments and scores). The post could be stressful; another advertisement from 1854 was placed by "an experienced *Kapellmeister*" who had had to give up his post for family reasons, but who now sought another. He could provide references and interested parties could apply to "H.K", Poste Restante, Grottkau, Bohemia.

One factor that might deter a candidate was that Austrian regiments frequently changed garrison and were rarely stationed in their home district. This was the Byzantine system (still used by the Turkish army until World War I), designed to ensure the troops' reliability; Czech soldiers were less likely to feel sympathy for Italian rioters, especially if they had not been in the area for long. Thanks to this system, Imperial Royal soldiers spent a great deal of their service on the march – in an empire largely bereft of railways and metalled roads. Between 1850 and 1855, the Italians of the 13th (Baron Wimpffen) Regiment were successively stationed in Terezin, Cesky Budovice, Klagenfurt, Eger, Zagreb, Udine, Trieste and Graz. None of these postings lasted more than a year and in 1851 and 1854, they changed garrison twice. The Moravians of the 54th (Prince Emil of Hesse) Regiment began 1850 in Gorizia, then moved to Trieste, ending the year in Hradec Kralove (Königgrätz). They moved to Vienna in 1851 and remained there until 1854, when they moved to Pest, then Transylvania, finally arriving in Brno in 1855. Their *Kapellmeister*, Wenzel Zavertal, who had joined in 1850, left in 1854 and his replacement is unknown. Josef Withe of the 13th, however, stayed at his post, completing 22 years service in 1866.

The *Kapellmeister*'s uniform made him a distinctive figure. His black tunic had collar and cuffs in his regiment's facing colour, (but no epaulettes) and his collar bore the badge of a crossed sword and lyre. His trousers were grey and he wore a silver and red waist sash and carried a sword with a silver and red knot. On parade he wore a cocked hat with black plumes and off parade he was entitled to an officer's forage cap.

Between 1850 and 1862, Austrian military music underwent a thorough reform – largely through the efforts of one man.

Andreas Leonhardt and his Reforms

In 1850, *Feldmarschalleutnant* Graf Degenfeld was ordered to reorganise the Austrian army's military bands and signals and to establish a comprehensive system of training and performance. Such a system was overdue, as bands had been allowed a great degree of freedom in previous years. In 1845, Wilhelm Wieprecht had observed the 64-strong band of the 7th (*Khevenhüller*) Infantry in Mainz and remarked that the brass instruments drowned the woodwind and that the bandsmen played the *forte* passages of a work better than the *piano*. The

Austria: the band of a 'German' infantry regiment, from a print by Trentsensky, 1855. The Drum Major is followed by the brass section.

The rest of the brass players and the percussionists. Note the 'basses', played with their bells facing to the rear.

The Kapellmeister (who actually marched on the right flank of the band) is followed by the woodwind and a rank of trumpeters.

differences between *hoboisten* and *bandisten* also troubled him. The most obvious were their uniforms: *hoboisten* wore far more braid and decoration and sometimes uniforms of a different colour. But, to Wieprecht, a greater problem lay in the *bandistens'* training; they were often technically competent, but no more and, in his opinion, such men "could not understand the spirit and character of [their] instrument and without this, [they] cannot completely master it." Another sign of how bands went their own way was in their marching pace, which varied from regiment to regiment and between 110 and 104 paces per minute.

Degenfeld, busy with a general reorganisation of the army, needed a capable man to carry out the new policy. A large number of potential candidates existed among serving or retired musicians, notably Josef Sawerthal and Philipp Fahrbach, but Degenfeld selected a fifty-year old composer and conductor who had dominated the musical life of Graz for over a decade. Andreas Leonhardt had served as a musician with several regiments and studied in Naples and Prague before becoming head of the Styrian Music Society in 1841. He had been a teacher, an organiser and a conductor of both orchestras and choirs; now he was summoned to Vienna to establish a new system as *Armeekapellmeister*, a post specially created for him. (He was also appointed *Kapellmeister* of the 60th (Vasa) Infantry, but it is doubtful how much time he was able to devote to this post, which he resigned in 1853).

The first signs of the new order came in a circular of April 8th, 1851, which established the strength of an infantry band at 48: 10 *hoboisten* (1 sergeant, 4 corporals and 5 lance-corporals) and 38 *bandisten* (all privates, up to twelve of whom were "pupil musicians" under training). The Drum Major now ranked officially as a warrant officer. The instrumentation was:

1 Piccolo 1 Flute 1 A Flat Clarinet 3 Clarinets in B 1 E Flat Clarinet
2 Bassoons 4 Horns 1 E Flat Cornet 2 Soprano Flugelhorns
1 Alto Flugelhorn 1 Bass Flugelhorn 1 Euphonium 1 "Obligato Trumpet"
4 E Flat Trumpets 1 "Bass Trumpet" 3 Trombones 2 "Basses"
Percussion: 2 Side Drums 2 Cymbal Players Bass Drum

A print by Trentsensky, published in 1855, shows a band on the march, led by two rows of six brass players – the "basses", played with their bells facing to the rear, are very prominent. They are followed by five percussionists, the *Kapellmeister* (who marched on the right flank of the band) and two ranks of six woodwind players, with a six man trumpet section bringing up the rear.

Jäger bands, like their Prussian counterparts, were all brass, with no percussion. Their strength was fixed at 24, but a photograph of the band of the 14th Battalion, taken in 1864, shows 43! How representative this was, I cannot say.

Cavalry bands also had a strength of 24, but this may not have always been achieved. Trentsensky shows both a cuirassier and a lancer band, both riding five abreast, with four trumpeters and the Trumpet Major leading the column. There are three ranks of bandsmen, with the bass instruments at the front, followed by trumpets, then horns and trombones.

The real shock in the circular was the abolition of the bands of the Artillery regiments with effect from May 1st, 1851. This reflected the reorganisation of the Artillery as a "mounted corps" with trumpeters, but the announcement caused a crisis at the Court Opera in Vienna, where the bandsmen of the 2nd

Austria: *Armeekapellmeister* (note the epaulettes), with the *Kapellmeister*, Drum Major and bandsmen of an infantry regiment. Print by Strassgschwandtner, 1854

Artillery Regiment had been an integral part of the orchestra for many years. A planned gala season was now in jeopardy and it took a petition to the Emperor by Bartholomeo Morelli, the opera's director, for the band to be reprieved – until the end of the season.

One significant step in Leonhardt's programme was the abolition of the elaborate uniforms worn by many *hoboisten*. Henceforth, all bandsmen would wear their regiment's uniform with "swallows nests" in the regimental colour, with "Imperial yellow" lace for privates and gold lace for NCOs. This helped break down the distinction between the two types of musicians and they were soon all being referred to as *bandisten*. At the same time, the Army was presented with a series of new bugle calls and drum beatings, although some signals, like the *Fussmarsch* of 1841, played by the company trumpeters to keep the step, were retained. (It is fair to assume that these signals were composed by Leonhardt.)

In the following years, Leonhardt inspected bands on a regular basis and introduced a regular system of scoring. He still found time to compose: in 1853, his *Alexander Cesarewitsch Marsch* was played before the Emperor, the Tsarevich and Friedrich Wilhelm IV of Prussia, who declared it was the best march he had heard in a long time. (It became a standard work in Prussia.) Nearly five years later, on January 18th, 1858, the funeral ceremony for Field Marshal Radetzky featured a march which made an impression on the British Ambassador, Horace Rumbold:

> Some resourceful bandmaster had had the simple but ingenious idea of setting Strauss's rousing "Radetzky March" in minor keys and at a funeral pace and as one regiment followed another, this melody rang like a dirge in the frosty air.

In fact Leonhardt had only used the familiar melody in the trio of his *Radetzkytrauermarsch*. Later that year another march celebrated the birth of Crown Prince Rudolf.

Like Wieprecht, Leonhardt was drawn to "monster concerts". In 1835, he had celebrated Emperor Ferdinand's visit to Graz with a concert involving the bands and drummers of seven regiments, the first time this had been done in Austria. The appointment as *Armeekapellmeister* gave him new opportunities and throughout the 1850s he assembled hundreds of musicians to celebrate the end of the annual manoeuvres or ceremonies such as the centenary of the Maria Theresia Order in June 1857. The tattoo held at Pest on 21st September 1852 featured ten infantry, four *Jäger* and two cavalry bands plus 100 drummers. A year later in Olmütz, the bands of thirteen infantry regiments, nine *Jäger* battalions and thirteen cavalry regiments, with 300 drummers were under his baton.

The disastrous war of 1859 meant that economies had to be made. When eighteen new infantry regiments were raised in 1860, their bands were only 32 strong and those of existing regiments were cut back. Two years later, Leonhardt retired on pension and the post of *Armeekapellmeister* disappeared for ever. He died in Vienna in 1866: it was the end of an era in more ways than one.

Regimental Marches

The story of the Imperial Royal Army's regimental music is a complicated one. Although a series of recordings of Austrian regimental marches has appeared in recent years, these are the marches in use at the end of the Empire and a glance at the listings in Eugen Brixel's authoritative work will show how often units changed their marches to reflect musical tastes, or their commanding officer's wishes. There was no Austrian equivalent of the Prussian Army March Collection and Emil Kaiser's *Sammlung von Armeemärsche und sonstige Kompositionen für das k.u.k Heer* (1895) is not really comparable. Even when Leonhardt ordered every infantry regiment to adopt a distinctive march, there were problems for the bandmasters; the new march had to be approved by the commanding officer, even if he had a "tin ear". Karl Leibold, the *Kapellmeister* of the 37th Infantry between 1848 and 1879, is reported to have had a particularly depressing experience when his C.O complained that a certain melody in the proposed regimental march was feeble, uninspiring – and too quiet. Suddenly, Leibold realised that the "Old Man" was referring to the trio, which contrasted with the bright, bold first subject. Shyly, he pointed out that "Er – that is the trio, Colonel." "Well, write a march with a <u>loud</u> trio, then!"

Relatively few marches from before 1867 have been recorded, but many of these are worth hearing. We can only hope that it will be possible one day to hear the *Coronini-Cronberg-Marsch* used by the 6th Infantry between 1851 and 1880, or Josef Gung'l's *Baron-Airoldi-Regimentsmarsch*, composed for the 23rd Regiment in the late 1850s. In the meantime, Chapter 4 contains a list of marches known to have been in use in 1866 and which were available as recordings at the time of writing.

The Austrian equivalent of "The British Grenadiers" or "Liliburlero" is the song *Prinz Eugen*, which commemorates Eugen of Savoy's campaign against the Turks in 1716 and which was the basis of Leonhardt's march of 1860. (The modern Federal Army's *Grosses Flaggenparade*, premiered in 1985, features the *Prinz-Eugen-Lied* in its opening section, with several other historical melodies.) The oldest infantry march is probably the 53rd's *Trenck-Panduren-Marsch*, which dates from the regiment's origin as a (very) irregular unit in 1741. The original melody is believed to have been composed by Baron von der Trenck himself. The 24th's *Strauch-Marsch* dates from 1809, while the 2nd's *Alexander-Marsch* is based on themes from the ballet *Der Blöde Ritter* ("The Idiot Knight") by the French composer Louis sur-Loiseau de Persius, which appeared around 1812. During the Congress of Vienna, Tsar Alexander I declared that it was his favourite march and "his" Austrian regiment was quick to adopt it. (The Prussians also took it up, as the *Wiener Alexander Marsch*). The period between 1815 and 1848 saw the appearance of the *Erzherzog-Carl-Marsch*, Johann Proksch's march for the 12th Regiment and the 18th's *Riesinger-Marsch* among others, while marches composed between 1848 and 1864 include the 40th's *Ritter-von-Rossbach-Marsch* and Carl Spohr's charming *Campagne-Marsch* for the 36th. An unusual march was composed by Wilhelm von Asboth of the 58th to celebrate his regiment's centenary; the *Wallonen-Marsch* is based on melodies from "Wallonia" (French-speaking Belgium), where the 58th was raised in 1763. Perhaps the most remarkable survival is the *45erKriegerklänge-Marsch* or *Sigmunds-Kriegerklänge-*

Marsch, composed in Bergamo around 1848, when the Archduke Sigismund Infantry was an Italian unit, recruited around Verona. After 1866, the regimental district was moved to Sanok in West Galicia, but the 45th retained this link to their Italian past until they were disbanded.

The abolition of *Jäger*, cavalry and artillery bands in 1868 meant that a large number of records were lost for good.Very little documentation of *Jäger* marches survives; Leonhardt wrote a *Kaiser Jäger-Marsch*, but neither this, nor the 10th Battalion's *Kopal-Jäger-Marsch* appears to have been recorded. Johann Strauss II's *Kaiser Jäger-Marsch* is a concert piece, guaranteed, (like most of Strauss's marches) to throw troops out of step.

Slightly more evidence exists for the cavalry. The 8th Cuirassiers, the oldest regiment in the army, used the *Pappenheimer-Marsch*, composed (probably by Michael Haydn) around 1790; the 1st Dragoons used "Prince Eugen" and the 5th (Radetzky) Hussars used – naturally – the "Radetzky". The 1st Lancers used Leonhardt's *Kronprinz-Rudolf-Marsch*, while the 3rd used the *Erzherzog-Carl-Marsch*.

The Artillery used the *Artillerie-Marsch* composed by Josef Dobyhall, the bandmaster of the 2nd Artillery Regiment and based on themes from Michael Balfe's opera "The Bohemian Girl" (*Die Zigeunerin* in German-speaking countries); Prince Wilhem of Prussia brought the score back from Vienna in 1841 and it became an Army March five years later. After 1860, it was the regimental march of the 4th (Queen's) Guard Grenadiers.

Trautenau, 27th June 1866: the 'drum dog' of the Archduke Carl Infantry (K.u.K. Inf. Rgt Nr 3). A detail from the painting by Fritz Neumann.

Austrian regimental marches of this period have a charm all their own and it is a pity that so few have been recorded.

Drum Majors and Drum Dogs

Although the *Kapellmeister* was in charge of the band, it was the Drum Major who was at its head on parade and on the march. Drum Majors were selected for their appearance; they had to be tall and dignified and were usually bearded. They ranked as warrant officers and could also be distinguished by a broad belt in the regimental facing colour, worn over the right shoulder. This was decorated with gold or silver lace, depending on the regiment's "button colour" and bore a small pair of ornamental drum sticks.

Another eye-catching sight was the bass drum, mounted on a two-wheeled cart and drawn by a large dog – often a St. Bernard – while the drummer marched behind. These "drum dogs" (*Paukenhunde*) first appeared in the 1850s (Brixel's work has no illustrations of them before this date) and it is not clear how many regiments had them. Nor is it clear how long the fashion lasted; by the turn of the century, many bands had their drum cart drawn by a pony, which may have been more reliable. Several regiments took their "drum dogs" on campaign; an engraving from the campaign in Denmark shows a group of musicians in greatcoats trudging through the rain, while the dog plods beside them, carrying the drumsticks in his mouth. A clue to why they fell out of favour is contained in Fritz Neumann's painting of the Archduke Carl Regiment's attack at Trautenau, where the dog is shown running off with the drum cart, with several soldiers in pursuit. Presumably the drummer (or the soldier told off as "dog handler") had been hit.

Two drum carts fell into Prussian hands after Königgrätz. One, of unknown provenance, was found by a patrol of the 8th Dragoons and presented to the 50th Regiment, who appear to have done little with it. However, as the 43rd Regiment advanced across the battlefield, they found the drum cart of the 77th (Archduke Carl Salvator) Regiment, with its dog lying dead in the shafts. Their trophy was soon a familiar sight in their garrison of Königsberg; the 43rd maintained two dogs, always named "Pasha" or "Sultan". (When they paraded before Emperor Franz Josef in 1895, the Austrian drum was replaced by a Prussian one.) In 1910, the band recorded the *Marsch des Prinz-August-Grenadier-Bataillon*, with interruptions by one of the dogs. This recording was released on a CD in 2005 (see "Recommended Recordings".) The 43rd was known throughout the army as the *Hundpauker* ("the Drum dogs") and the tradition was carried on by their successors in the Reichswehr and Wehrmacht-Heer.

An Unrequited Love Affair

Between 1817 and 1866, no less than thirty-four marches of Austrian origin – or on Austrian themes – were added to the Prussian Army's march collection. Several, including most of the regimental marches, were brought back from state visits by the royal family. In 1835, for example, Prince Wilhelm heard the march of the 25th (von Trapp) Regiment in Prague and asked for the score; the same thing happened when he visited "his" regiment, the 34th, in Olmütz eighteen years later. Both became Army Marches.

Austria: Drum Major and bandsman of the 27th (Leopold, King of
the Belgians) Infantry in full dress, photographed in 1864.

A second reason was the Kaiser Franz Grenadier Regiment, formed in 1814
and named after Prussia's ally in the War of Liberation – a title it retained after
the emperor died in 1835. The regiment maintained strong links with Austria and
its band made a speciality of "Austrian" music, especially under the leadership
of August-Heinrich Neithardt and Wilhelm Christoph. Austrian composers
were always welcome in Berlin: Josef Gung'l worked there in the 1840s (and saw
three of his compositions become Army Marches), while the Strauss family could
always guarantee that their concerts would sell out. And in 1914, five of the eight

infantry regiments in the Berlin garrison had "Austrian" regimental marches. But this remained a one-sided affair: Prussian marches were rarely, if ever, heard in Vienna.

In November 1864, the 34th (Wilhelm I, King of Prussia's) Regiment, returning from the campaign in Schleswig, were invited to Berlin by their Colonel-in-Chief. On the 21st, King Wilhelm led the regiment through the city and its colours were lodged in the Royal Palace. Next day, the King, wearing the regiment's uniform, took the salute as they marched down Unter den Linden (a scene captured in a painting by Carl Röchling). During the parade, the 34th's band, under Sigmund Levengly, played a new march, *Ungarn und Brandenburg*. Afterwards, the officers were guests at a banquet in the palace and Wilhelm then visited the men, who danced the *Krakowiak*, a dance from their home district of Kaschau in Slovakia. Later, the king asked Friedrich Wilhelm Voigt, Bandmaster of the First Foot Guards, to compose a march with the *Krakowiak* in the trio.

To anyone aware of what lay ahead for the King of Prussia's Regiment, this march will arouse mixed – and uncomfortable – feelings.

A piano version of the best known march of the era and a regular feature of the New Year's Concert from Vienna (complete with the correct drumbeat). A month after Johann Strauss I's death on September 25th, 1849, the King of Prussia commanded it become an Army March. The first arrangement was by Wilhelm Christoph of the Kaiser Franz Grenadiers; it was his regiment's quick march until 1919.

Chapter 3

Musicians at War: The Campaign of 1866

In Summer 1866, both the Prussian and Austrian armies took their bands on campaign and they feature in many illustrations, while historians describe how regiments advanced with their bands playing. Yet there is very little hard evidence of what was actually played – our glimpses of musicians on the battlefield are fragmentary and accounts are often unreliable. What makes this surprising is that the previous European war can claim to be one of the most "musical" in history.

1864: the War with Denmark

Both the Saxon and Hanoverian troops sent to Holstein by the German Confederation in December 1863 and the Prussian and Austrian regiments who arrived a few weeks later were accompanied by their bands, who performed on parade and on the march, gave concerts and did their best for their comrades' – and the civilians' – morale. A large number of marches were composed; the Austrian commander, Gablenz, was the subject of no less than six, two of which became Austrian regimental marches. Other marches commemorated the action of Lundby and the capture of Alsen, while the crossing of the Lymfjord was the subject of both a Prussian and an Austrian march. (The Austrian, by Franz Scharoch, was originally the *Dormus-Marsch*, after the commander of the Austrian 4th Brigade, but in 1889, General Dormus requested a change of title,

Düppel, April 18th, 1864: Gottfried Piefke conducts his bandsmen under fire.

Austria: Drummer, 80th (Prince Wilhelm of Schleswig-Holstein-Glücksberg's) Infantry Regiment on campaign in Demark 1864, by Herbert Knötel.

Prussia: Bandsman, 2nd Foot Guards on campaign in 1866. Based on an eye-witness sketch from *Der Soldatenfreund*.

to honour his men, rather than himself.) In Vienna, Johann Strauss wrote the *Verbrüderungs* ("Brotherhood") march and followed it with *Deutsche Krieger* ("German Warriors"), while Verdi celebrated the Austrian victory at Oversee with a march he later recycled in *Aida*. But the most famous musical incident involved Gottfried Piefke and his role in the capture of Düppel.

Early on the morning of April 18th, as the troops prepared to assault the Danish redoubts, four bands (around a hundred and fifty men) assembled in the reserve trenches. Piefke climbed up onto what appears (in a contemporary illustration) to be a barrel and prepared to conduct with a drawn sword, to which he had attached a small Prussian flag. At 10 o'clock, a rocket signalled the assault and, as the storming parties left the trenches, the bands struck up Beethoven's *Marsch des Yorck'schen Korps*, a popular march from the War of Liberation. This was followed, apparently, by Piefke's march on themes from Gounod's *Faust* (known as *Margarethe* in Germany), which had cheered the Brandenburg regiments at the previous autumn's manoeuvres. Nobody recorded what the bands were playing when a Danish shell burst on the parapet, blocked several instruments with earth and (according to Piefke) cut the music off far more abruptly than any conductor could have done. However, no one was injured and the bands were soon playing again. As Prussian flags appeared on one redoubt after another, Piefke ordered his men to play fanfares and – only then – was persuaded to descend from his

Trautenau, June 27th, 1866: General Gablenz sends in Grivicic's Brigade, accompanied by its bands.

Austrian bandsmen in bivouac, July 1866.

precarious perch. Later, the bands played *Now thank we all our God* and the Prussian national anthem in a captured redoubt.

Afterwards, Piefke would commemorate the "near miss" in his *Düppler-Marsch*, but there is no evidence that his better-known *Düppler-Schanzen-Sturmmarsch* ("The Storming of Düppel") was played during the assault, although it may have been composed beforehand. (The first definite performance was given at Flensburg station on April 21st, when the king arrived to visit his troops.) Five of Piefke's marches in the Army Collection date from this campaign, although they are unlikely to have gained general currency by 1866.

1866: the Early Battles

In his *Tactical and General Instructions*, issued to the Imperial Royal Northern Army in May 1866, Feldzeugmeister Ludwig von Benedek found time to set out his views on the role of military musicians:

> The members of the bands are not to be considered merely as musicians for service in peace; they are no less than soldiers, whose function is to cheer and encourage their comrades. They are therefore not to be sent to the rear at the beginning of an engagement; their place in action is with the main body of their corps – as they share the dangers, so will they also share the glory.

Earlier, Benedek had criticised the Prussians' dependence on musketry and declared: "An energetic dash _____ will, against Prussian troops, always bring about success most rapidly and completely."

There are no references to military bands in any of Helmuth von Moltke's plans or orders for the campaign.

The fighting that erupted on June 27th gives tantalising glimpses of musicians in action. At Trautenau, where Gablenz's X Corps advanced against the Prussian I Corps, the brigades of Wimpffen and Grivicic went into action with their bands playing the *Radetzkymarsch*, but were unsuccessful. The last reserve, Knebel's brigade, deployed straight from its line of march and moved against the *Kapellenberg* (Chapel Hill), with the 1st (Emperor Franz Josef) Regiment in the first line and the Archduke Carl Regiment in support. The latter regiment's band played the "Radetzky" during the attack. After several failed attempts, the 1st Regiment secured the position, while the Archduke Carl Regiment, moving to their flank, attacked from another direction. Their casualties were relatively light, although, as we have seen, the "drum dog" made a bolt for freedom. The "Kaiser Infantry" were hard hit, however, and the band were involved: Drum Major Ratengruber threw away his staff, took a rifle from a wounded man and attached himself to the 6th Company. Afterwards, the men stood bareheaded while the surviving bandsmen played the National Anthem. It had been a victory, but a costly one – the Austrians lost nearly four times as many men as the Prussians and the "Kaiser Infantry" alone suffered four hundred casualties – the band lost two men dead and six wounded. Thanks to poor staff work, Gablenz's corps would suffer disaster the following day.

The action at Trautenau began hours after another had ended. For most of the morning Ramming's VI Corps had launched repeated attacks against the Prussian positions west of Nachod and around the village of Wysokow. Here, too, a drum major had abandoned his role in the heat of action. As Major General von Ollech, the commander of the Prussian advanced guard, rode forward to observe the attack of Jonak's brigade, he was spotted by a mounted officer of the 14th *Jäger* Battalion. Ollech's epaulettes marked him out as a "priority target"; the officer rode into his battalion's skirmish line, cheerfully called out to his men and pointed to Ollech, who fell, hit by two bullets. Seeing this, Sergeant Drummer Braun, the Drum Major of the 2nd Battalion, 58th Regiment, snatched a rifle from a private, aimed and shot the officer from the saddle – which gained him the General Military Decoration 3rd Class. Ollech was seriously wounded, but survived (against all expectations); the identity of the *Jäger* officer is not known for certain, but he was probably the 14th's Commanding Officer, Major Jesovits, who was reported killed in this action.

The following day, the Prussians advanced further west and encountered Archduke Leopold's VII Corps at Skalitz. Benedek had ordered the Archduke to avoid an engagement, but Leopold's subordinates decided to respond to the Prussian advance with a frontal attack. As General Gustav Fragnern's brigade moved off, the band of the 77th (Archduke Carl Salvador) Regiment played Carl Faust's *Glück Auf!*, a march based on traditional miners' songs. Fragnern launched his brigade against the Prussians in Dubno Wood and within a quarter of an hour, he and many of his men were dead. The 77th later adopted *Glück Auf!* as their regimental march, rechristening it the *Skalitz-Marsch*.

The final "musical example" from this phase of the campaign comes from the action of Gitschin on the 29th. Piret's brigade (the 29th *Jäger* Battalion and the 18th (Grand Prince Constantine) and 45th (Archduke Sigismund) Regiments) were sent to recapture the village of Diletz; Theodor Fontane tells us that one column advanced "with bands playing", while a second went forward to the anthem *Gott erhalte unser Kaiser*, (though Haydn's beautiful melody is difficult to march to). The attack, however, failed. Reliance on "an energetic dash" was proving hideously costly – and unsuccessful.

Königgrätz

The decisive battle of the war began in mist and drizzle and a similar "mist" seems to hang around the part played by musicians. There are plenty of anecdotes, but little evidence to confirm them. In his history of the war, Theodor Fontane quotes some of the stories that circulated after the battle:

> _____ a drummer who had lost his drumsticks, but continued to beat the "Charge" with bloody fingers; or an entire band, surrounded in the woods, that had cut their way out with their tubas and trombones.

Fontane used this second story as the basis for his poem *Die Gardemusik bei Chlum*, where a band "forms square" while Hungarian hussars hack at their instruments, before retiring. (The only "fatality" is the bassoon.) As Fontane does not identify the band, one cannot say whether the story is true or not. There are, however, two definite examples of "music on the battlefield" from the Prussian side.

The 57th are Played into Action

The Prussian Elbe Army's advance against the Austrian left (held by the Saxon Corps) was a cautious one and it was not until after 2pm that the 28th Brigade (17th & 57th Regiments) crossed the Bistritz and advanced on Problus. In charge of the skirmishers of the 2nd Company, 57th Regiment was Ensign Fritz Hönig, who would later become a well-known (and controversial) military historian and who left a vivid account of what happened.

Once the brigade had deployed, with two battalions of the 57th in the first line and two battalions of the 17th in support, the commander, General Heller ordered Colonel von der Osten of the 57th to advance. The plateau ahead was covered in standing rye the height of a man, soaked by the recent rain (afterwards, Hönig recorded, the troops looked as though they had dived into a river) and only the mounted officers could see over it; von der Osten was told to make for Popowitz Wood, then to take the church tower in Problus as his objective. The colours were uncased, the order was given "Brigade – March" and the bands of both regiments began to play. The brigade advanced over wet ground and through the rye – and under a sporadic artillery fire – but the bands kept playing until they were 250 yards from the Saxons in Briz Wood, as Hönig (who was close to his own regiment's band) recorded:

> The music was quite steady – and it only ceased when 2/57th was extended. The last march played by the band of the 57th was the men's favourite one and they were accustomed to fill up the recurrent pauses between the phrases, breaking in with "Oh, Hannes, what a hat!" [*In Low German dialect "O Hannes, wat en Haut!" – RM*]

The enemy was only visible to the mounted officers and *Stabshoboist* Northe was unable to hear his C.O's shouts of "Stop!" until the Saxons opened fire.

> The music stopped almost by common consent –––– However, the enemy, not the *Stabshoboist*, had given the signal. The latter looked about him in vexation, while Colonel von der Osten's voice was heard saying "Northe, stop it!" at the same moment the band ceased.

Hönig suggests that the 57th hadn't shaken off peace-time habits, but the band was doing its job rather well, keeping the men together in difficult conditions and playing familiar tunes to bolster morale. (What a shame that Hönig doesn't identify them.) As the brigade crossed the heights of Popowitz, the whole battlefield became visible:

> As far as the view ranged, there were skirmishers and columns advancing, colours flying and music playing – I have never seen anything which approached this battlepiece in its effect on the imagination.

Morale, which was already good, soared; the 28th Brigade went forward and carried all its objectives. But the principal musical incident of the battle had already taken place – and it had involved Gottfried Piefke.

A Boost for Royal Morale

Around 1.30pm, Royal Headquarters, sharing the Roskoberg hill with First Army's headquarters, was becoming prey to doubt. The First Army had been in action for several hours, but the Austrians were gradually pushing them out of the Hola and Swiep Woods; the Elbe Army on the Prussian right flank was moving sluggishly and there was no sign of the Second Army on the left flank. Only Moltke seemed calm and confident, resisting all attempts to commit the First Army's reserves, the Brandenburgers of the 5th and 6th Divisions. At one point, he rode away from the Staff, hoping, perhaps, that no decision could be made without him. However, the commander of the First Army, Prince Friedrich Karl, took this opportunity to order the 5th Division forward. Leading the division were the 8th Grenadiers with Gottfried Piefke; their march would take them past the King on the Roskoberg and. Piefke ordered his men to play one of the stock pieces in their repertoire, Josef Golde's *Preussenmarsch* (*Marsch über National-Melodien*), whose first subject is the Prussian national anthem, *Heil Dir im Siegerkranz* ("Hail, crowned with victory"), which uses the same melody as *God save the Queen*. It had an immediate effect on the King's morale, as he later wrote to his wife:

> These were anxious times and I was uncertain how things would turn out. Then Piefke and the Leib-Regiment came past and I suddenly heard the National Anthem. That was an inspiring moment.

The King's doubts finally vanished when the Crown Prince's Second Army began to attack the Austrian flank. In fact, the 5th Division saw very little action; total casualties for the 8th Grenadiers were eighteen other ranks wounded, a fraction of the losses at Gitschin on June 29th, or in the cholera epidemic at the end of the war. After the battle, Piefke was present as the King, riding through his cheering troops, encountered the Crown Prince. Once again, the 8th's bandsmen played *Heil Dir im Siegerkranz* and the King told their conductor "Piefke, I will never forget what you did today."

Later, Piefke assembled three bands and performed a new march before the King and the staff. Three encores were demanded and *Der Königgrätzer* became an Army March almost immediately, with the proviso that it could not be played on large scale parades! This was because Piefke had used the *Hohenfriedberg March* in the trio and this eighteenth century melody, the march of the Ansbach-Bayreuth Dragoons, had passed to their successors, the 2nd (Queen's) Cuirassiers, who disapproved of any other unit using it. (When Piefke wrote a version for cavalry band, he composed a new trio.) It is often claimed that Piefke composed the march on the battlefield, but this seems unlikely, considering the problems of actually writing a score and copying band parts in a muddy field during a battle. It is far more probable that, as with his earlier "Düppel" march, Piefke had kept the score by him and awaited the opportunity to "christen" it. That night, as the Prussians bivouacked on the battlefield, their bands played *Now Thank We All Our God*.

Death March

It is difficult to give an account of the Austrian bands at Koniggrätz, because the evidence is so fragmentary and confined to anecdotes, such as the story of Drummer Georg Fallesch of the 47th (Ritter von Hartung) Regiment, who was wounded in the hand, but continued to beat the charge until he fainted from loss of blood. And when Rosenzweig's brigade was launched against Rosberitz, the horn players of the 17th *Jäger* Battalion sounded the charge, while the band of the Hoch-und-Deutschmeister Regiment played the Austrian anthem. But most accounts simply describe regiments advancing "with bands playing" and – once again – the only march mentioned is the "Radetzky". No doubt this familiar tune, a reminder of the glory days of 1848–1849, was played in action – but how often? That question remains unanswered.

In his *Mir San von k.u.k* – Stefan Vadja paints a vivid picture of bands accompanying their regiments into the inferno, with snatches of the "Radetzky" – sometimes played by the brass, sometimes by the woodwind – drifting back as the ranks are torn apart "like a ghastly parody of Haydn's *Farewell Symphony*, where the instruments fall silent one after the other." The bandsmen, sent in to inspire their comrades, were dying beside them.

Sometime during the last assault on Chlum, the King of Prussia's Regiment, who we last saw on parade in Berlin, advanced into a narrow lane that became known as *Der Hohlweg der Toten* ("Dead Man's Lane") and were caught in a cross fire. They suffered 1580 casualties and the survivors formed a single battalion.

There were lighter moments: Eugen Brixel describes a long-serving (anonymous) *Kapellmeister* who led his band away from the front line and placed them in cover behind a barn, where they were surprised by the enemy. The Prussians' commanding officer asked the startled Austrian to play a Strauss waltz for him and his officers, as they might never have a chance to hear "one of Austria's famous military bands" again. The Austrians obliged, with the din of battle in the background and were wildly applauded.

Brixel does not name the *Kapellmeister*, presumably because he was technically guilty of desertion. But his band – unlike many of their fellow musicians – survived intact.

Piefkes on Parade

The Prussians never entered Vienna, but on July 31st, the First Army paraded at Ganserdorf on the Marschfeld, twenty kilometres North West of the city, with St Stephen's Cathedral clearly visible on the horizon. That day, King Wilhelm wore the uniform of Colonel-in-Chief of the 8th Grenadiers and when the infantry marched past in column of companies, the 9th Brigade (8th Grenadiers and 48th Infantry) was the leading unit. Their bands led them to the reviewing point, then wheeled to the left to play them past.

Hundreds of Viennese had come to see the parade and there was loud speculation about the two men – one stocky, with a bristling moustache and eyebrows, the other over six feet tall, broad-shouldered and with a full beard

– who were leading the bands. The troops on crowd control recognised them, however and the word was passed along: "Die Piefkes kommen!" This struck a chord with the Austrians; thanks to Gottfried and Rudolf, North Germans, especially Prussians, have been "Piefkes" ever since.

Meanwhile the Prussian Guards had occupied Prague and the officers of the Kaiser Franz Guard Grenadiers made no secret of the fact that Franz Josef was their respected Colonel-in-Chief. The regimental history states that this ensured good relations with the inhabitants and *Stabshoboist* Heinrich Saro's concerts drew large crowds.

An armistice had been signed at Nikolsburg on July 26th and by the end of the year, most of the Prussian army had returned home. The musical "consequences" of this German civil war were largely confined to the Austrians; despite the opposition of Archduke Albrecht and many senior officers, the bands of the *Jägers*, cavalry and artillery were abolished on February 22nd, 1868. (The white coats of the Austrian infantry had already been replaced, after nearly two hundred years, by blue and some conservatives were grumbling about "Franz Josef the Abolitionist"). In Prussia, Gottfried Piefke was the musical "star" of the campaign; but Wilhelm Wieprecht was on the verge of his greatest triumph.

1866 was the last time that military bands appeared on the battlefield *en masse*. In the War of 1870-1871, Prussian bands would almost always be on the sidelines: on August 6th, 1870, the band of the 50th Infantry played marches and patriotic airs as the men of the Third Army marched up to the firing line, but they did not follow them. As Ensign Hönig and that anonymous *Kapellmeister* had realised, their future role would be confined to concerts and ceremonial roles.

Zur

Feier des 50jährigen Stiftungs-Festes

des

I. Garde-Dragoner-Regiments

am 21. Februar 1865.

PROGRAMM.

1) Hohenfriedberger Marsch.

2) **Marsch. Zum 21. Februar**, componirt von Seiner Königlichen Hoheit dem Prinzen Albrecht (Sohn) von Preussen.

3) Ouvertüre zur Oper: „Die Stumme von Portici," von Auber.

4) Walzer aus der Oper: „Margarethe," von Gounod.

5) Marsch aus der Oper: „Nurmahal," von Spontini.

6) Husaren-Lied aus der Oper: „Ein Feldlager," von Spontini.

7) Der Traum, Walzer von Dahse.

8) Torgauer Marsch.

9) Centifolien-Polka-Mazurka von Fliege.

Druck von Ernst Litfass, Königlichem Hofbuchdrucker, Adlerstr. 6.

The programme of a concert to celebrate the Prussian 1st Guard Dragoons' 50th birthday. For some reason, they played the *Hohenfriedberger*, which the 2nd Cuirassiers regarded as their private property (see p.38) and not the *Kavallerie-Marsch* (AM III/21) composed for them by Wieprecht and used by them since 1836. The *Torgauer Marsch*, often ascribed to Frederick the Great, was in fact composed in Torgau around 1816, by a teacher named Scholz . It was brought to Prussia by King Friedrich Wilhelm III in 1817 and was a favourite in the royal family, but did not become an Army March until 1891!

Chapter 4

The Repertoire

Much of the music played in 1866 is available on record but production companies and conductors prefer to stick to familiar material. A more adventurous choice of music would give a better idea of the contemporary repertoire, especially the Austrian. These notes will, I hope, help to identify this material.

Prussia
Marches from before 1815
AM I/1 *Marsch in Es* (Friedrich II)
AM I/1a *Präsentiermarsch* (Friedrich Wilhelm III)
AM I/1b *Der Dessauer* (Anon)
AM I/1d *Der Rheinströmer* (Anon)
AM I/1e *Mollwitzer Marsch* (Friedrich II)
AM I/1f *Marsch 1756* (Friedrich II)
AM I/7 *Marsch I Bataillon Garde* (1806) (Anon)
AM I/9 *Marsch Herzog von Braunschweig* (Anon)
AM I/10 *Marsch Prinz August Grenadier Bataillon* (Müller)
AM I/24 *Alter russischer Marsch* (Glück)
AM I/ 27 *Der Coburger* (M. Haydn)
AM I/30 *Marsch des Leib-Garde-Preobaschenski-Regiments* (Anon)
AM II/37 *Marsch des Yorck'schen Korps* (Beethoven)
AM II/38 *Pariser Einzugsmarsch* (Walch)
AM II/41 *Wiener Alexander-Marsch* (Persius)

Marches from 1815-1866
AM II/58 *Marsch nach Motiven der Oper "Moses" von Rossini* (Widder)
AM II/62 *Marsch des Leib-Garde-Semeneovski-Regiments* (Anon)
AM II/73 *Marsch von Kronprinzen aus Italien mitgebracht* (Anon)
AM II/113 *Marsch 1837 aus Petersburg* (Anon)
AM II/118 *Marsch nach Motiven der Oper "Die Hugenotten" von Meyerbeer* (Hubner)
AM II/119 *Preussenmarsch (Marsch über National-Melodien)* (Golde)
AM II/123 *Marsch des russischen Grenadier-Regiments Konig Friedrich Wilhelm III* (Anon)
AM II/124 *Marsch nach Motiven der Oper "Die Regimentstochter" von Donizetti* (Anon)
AM II/126 *Geschwindmarsch nach Motiven von Quadrillen von Johann Strauss* (Christoph)
AM II/131 *Geschwindmarsch* (von Redern)
AM II/136 *Marsch nach Motiven der Oper "Die Zigeunerin" von Michael Balfe* (Dobyhall)

AM II/137 *Pochhammer-Marsch* (Piefke)
AM II/141 *Oesterreichischer Defiliermarsch* (Strauss)
AM II/145 *Radetzky-Marsch* (Strauss)
AM II/155 *Marsch nach Motiven der Oper "Indra" von Flotow* (Neumann)
AM II/160 *Pepita-Marsch* (Pfeifke)
AM II/161 *Alexander-Marsch* (Leonhardt)
AM II/163 *Marsch* (von Redern)
AM II/164 *Gitana-Marsch* (Piefke)
AM II/165 *Geschwindmarsch* (von Redern)
AM II/166 *Geschwindmarsch uber den Kölner Dombaulied* (Laudenbach)
AM II/178 *Fahnenweihemarsch* (Löwenthal)
AM II/180 *Angriffskolonnen-Marsch* (Voigt)
AM II/182 *Margarethen-Marsch* (Piefke)
AM II/184 *Liechtenstein-Marsch* (Strauss)

Prize marches from Bote & Bock's competitions
AM II/157 *Kolonnenmarsch* (Winter)
AM II/158 *Marsch nach Motiven der Oper "Grossfürstin Sophia Catherina" von
    Flotow* (Meinberg)
AM II/168 *Defiliermarsch* (Faust)
AM II/169 *Manövriermarsch* (Winter)
AM II/172 *Prinz-Friedrich-Wilhelm-Marsch* (Saro)
AM II/173 *Helenenmarsch* (Lubbert)
AM II/174 *Viktoriamarsch* (Neumann)
AM II/175 *Soldatenklänge* (Buchholtz)
AM II/176 *Defiliermarsch* (Saro)

Cavalry marches
AM III/ 1b *Der Hohenfriedberger*
Sechs Märsche fur Kavallerie-Musik (Wieprecht)
AM III/21 *Kavallerie-Marsch* (Wieprecht)
AM III/29 *Marsch zur Fest der weissen Rose* (von Redern)
AM III/37 *Trabmarsch nach Motiven des Ballets "Giselle" von Adolphe Adam*
    (Lorenz)
AM III/51 *Parademarsch Nr. 1* (Möllendorf)
AM III/55 *Parademarsch* (Princess Elisabeth of Saxe-Meiningen)
AM III/61 *Viktoria-Marsch* (Wieprecht)

Austria
Some of these marches were added to the Prussian collection and include their
AM number. The date in brackets indicates the first mention of the march; the
actual date of composition may have been earlier.
Anonymous: *Erzherzog-Carl-Marsch* (1822) AM II/51
Gyulai-Marsch (pre-1835)
Jellacic-Marsch (1849)
Marsch des Regiments Prinz von Preussen (pre-1853) AM II/159
Riesinger-Marsch (1841) AM II/139

Strauch-Marsch (1809)
Trenck-Panduren-Marsch (c1741)
Asboth, Wilhelm von *Wallonen-Marsch* (1863)
Erkel, Ferenc *Hunyadi-Marsch* (1846)
Faust, Georg *Skalitz-Marsch* (pre-1866)
Gung'l, Josef *Kriegers Lust* (1844) A M II/ 127
Jeschko, Ludwig *Rekruten-Marsch* (1857) AM II/171
Leonhardt, Andreas *Alexander-Cesarewitsch-Marsch* (1853) AM II/161
Kronprinz-Rudolf-Marsch (1858)
Prinz-Eugen-Marsch (1860)
Retraite und Zapfenstreich zu Olmütz (1853)
Massak, Franz *Freiherr-von-Hess-Marsch* (c1850)
Matuscka, J Leopold *Ritter-von-Rossbach-Marsch* (aka *40er-Defiliermarsch*) (1852)
Muller, Josef *Offiziersregiments-Marsch* (pre-1856)
Oldrini, Giovanni *Franz-Josef-Marsch* (1852) AM II/154
Persuis, Louis de *Alexander-Marsch* (c.1814) AM II/41
Proksch, Josef *Marsch des Regiments Graf Rothkirch* (1836) AM II/107
Scharoch, Franz *Lymfjord-Marsch* (originally "*Dormus-Marsch*") (1864)
Sechter, Eduard *Gablenz-Marsch* (1864)
Spohr, Karl *Campagne-Marsch* (c1850-1852)
Stenzl, C F *Gablenz-Marsch* (1864)
Swoboda, Franz Wolfgang *Radetzky-Sieges-Marsch* (1848)
Tischler, Anton *Sommacampagna-Marsch* (c1848-1849)
Toman, Franz *Concordia-Marsch* (1851)
Zawerdal, A *45er Kriegerklänge-Marsch* (a.k.a *Sigmunds-Kriegerklänge-Marsch*)
    (1848)
And –
Strauss, Johann *Radetzky-Marsch* (1849)

Music inspired by the campaign

Relatively few marches commemorating what was seen by many as a fratricidal war entered the Prussian Collection: the best known, after Piefke's *Königgrätzer*, is the *Steinmetz-Marsch* (AM II 197) by Carl Bratfisch, the *Stabshoboist* of the 58th Infantry, which commemorates the action of Skalitz and has remained popular ever since. Less well known, but equally good is Heinrich Laudenbach's *Marsch von Problus und Prim am 3 Juli 1866* (AM II 194) and the marches by Piefke which were never taken into the collection.

There are – understandably – very few Austrian marches inspired by the campaign in Bohemia; Josef Strauss's *Benedek-Marsch* was composed for a fund-raising concert in Vienna in late June, but the concert (postponed twice by bad weather) was overtaken by events and there is no evidence the piece was performed. Josef Preiss's *Trautenau-Gefechts-Marsch* had better luck; this tribute to the "Kaiser-Infantry" became their regimental march. The successful campaign against Italy was a more fruitful source of music.

Chapter 5

Personalities

I t is relatively easy to find biographical information on the commanders (and their subordinates) on both sides in the 1866 campaign. Musicians, however, are rarely mentioned. I hope these brief biographical sketches will restore the balance.

Wilhelm Christoph (1810–1859)

Christoph joined the band of the Kaiser Franz Grenadiers in 1828 and by 1840 was its principal clarinettist. When August-Heinrich Neithardt (q.v.) resigned in that year, he recommended Christoph as his successor; the next few years would prove him right. As bandmaster of the Emperor of Austria's "personal" Prussian regiment, Christoph continued to add to the regiment's "Austrian" repertoire. His first significant composition was his *Geschwindmarsch nach Motiven aus Quadrillen von Johann Strauss*, which is often ascribed to Strauss himself. (In fact, Christoph had arranged themes from two Strauss quadrilles note for note.) Christoph also composed a march based on Josef Labitsky's *Jasminwalzer* and one on themes composed by King Georg V of Hanover and arranged several Austrian marches for Prussian military band, notably Johann Strauss I's *Oesterreichischer Defiliermarsch* and *Radetzkymarsch* and Giovanni Oldrini's *Franz-Josef-Marsch*. A sign of the esteem in which he was held came in 1853, when he accompanied Friedrich Wilhelm IV to Vienna – a rare honour for an NCO! One consequence was his arrangement of Leonhardt's *Alexander-Cesarewitsch-Marsch*.

This talented musician died of smallpox in 1859 and was succeeded by Heinrich Saro (q.v.). He left a lasting influence on Prussian military music; in 1914, five of the Berlin Guards regiments had "Austrian" regimental marches and all but one were composed or arranged by Wilhem Christoph.

Philipp Fahrbach Senior (1815–1885)

Born in Vienna, Fahrbach was trained as a flautist by his brother Josef, before joining Johann Strauss I's orchestra. The two men were soon friends. He formed his own orchestra at the age of 21 and in 1838, when Strauss was on a concert tour, he led the music for the Court Ball season – despite being a Protestant.

Fahrbach served as *Kapellmeister* of the Hoch-und-Deutschmeister regiment between 1841 and 1846, then returned to civilian life. Between 1850 and 1856, he and Johann Strauss II took turns conducting the music for Court Balls, but in the latter year, he became Bandmaster of the 14th (Grand Duke of Hesse's) Regiment. The "Hessians" took part in the campaigns of 1859 (Fahrbach and his men helped care for the wounded after Solferino) and 1864; Fahrbach retired in 1865 and devoted himself to dance music.

Fahrbach's compositions include the *Brigade-Marsch*, *Cremona-Marsch*, *Baron-Hess-Marsch* and *Erinnerungen an Magenta*. His son, Philipp Junior (1843–1894) served as a bandmaster in the 1870s.

Carl Faust's *Glück Auf* was known as the *Skalitz-Marsch* in Austria. Here
is a piano reduction by Karl Masa, bandmaster of the 77th Regiment
who had played it as the Regiment advanced on June 28th 1866.

Carl Faust (1825–1892)

This prolific composer was a Silesian, born in Neisse. He first came to public
notice in 1856, when he was serving as *Stabshoboist* of the 36th Infantry, in the
Federal fortress of Luxembourg and his *Defiliermarsch* gained First Prize in Bote
& Bock's competition. It became an Army March in the following year and
has remained in the repertoire ever since. In 1859, Faust transferred to the 11th
Infantry in Breslau and in 1865 he moved to the 3rd (Queen Elisabeth's) Guard
Grenadiers who were, at that time, stationed in the same city. He retired in 1869,
and later worked with various bands and orchestras in Silesia.

Faust was a popular composer of dance music – one of his polkas (indirectly)
provoked Gottfried Piefke to a memorable rage – but he was also well known for
his marches. These include *Glück Auf!* ("Take care!"), based on Silesian miners'

songs, which became very popular in Saxony and Austria (where it was known as the *Skalitz-Marsch*), the *Loigny-Marsch* for the 90th (Mecklenburg) Fusiliers, commemorating an action in the Franco-German war, a cavalry trot, *Die Marketendrin* ("The Sutleress"), the cavalry gallop *Wo lustig die Hörner erschallen* ("Where the (hunting) horns cheerfully sound") and a celebratory march for Wilhelm Wieprecht's Silver Jubilee as Inspector of Music, which was played as part of the serenade outside his lodgings.

Josef Golde (1802-1886)

Golde, a Thuringian, was 24 when he joined the 32nd Infantry in Erfurt, becoming its *Stabshoboist* the following year. He was a prominent figure in the city's musical life; besides composing marches and cantatas, he gave piano, violin and singing lessons and was head of the city's musical society. In 1840, his *Preussenmarsch* (*Marsch über National-Melodien*), based on the Prussian national anthem and with the patriotic song *Ich bin ein Preusse* in the trio, became an Army March and remained in the repertoire for many years. In 1851, Golde became a Royal Prussian Music Director and in 1858, he created the *Festreveille*, incorporating the chorale *Nun danket alle Gott*, sung by Frederick the Great's army after the battle of Leuthen on November 5th, 1757. This became an important part of the ceremony of the *Grosses Wecken* (Long Reveille), performed every New Year's Day and on the Sovereign's birthday.

Josef Gung'l (1810-1889)

Born at Szambek in Hungary, Gung'l joined the 5th Artillery Regiment in Pest in 1828, then transferred to the 4th Artillery in Graz, becoming their *Kapellmeister*. He left the army in 1843 and was employed by Bote & Bock in Berlin; the following year, a collection of his marches was published. Three of these were added to the Prussian collection in 1846 and he became an honorary Royal Prussian Music Director in 1849.

Gung'l formed his own orchestra and led it on a series of tours, notably to the USA in 1848-1849 (where he conducted at President Zachary Taylor's inauguration) and Russia, where he performed regularly at St. Petersburg and Pavlovsk between 1850 and 1855. In 1856, he returned to the army as *Kapellmeister* of the 23rd (Baron Airoldi) Regiment and held this post until 1864. His "comeback" as a civilian composer was unsuccessful; this field was now dominated by Johann Strauss II and Offenbach and Gung'l finally retired to Weimar.

Gung'l's compositions, popular in their day, are now little known, but his march *Kriegers Lust* (Warrior's Delight) was both a Prussian Army march and the march of the Arad Volunteers in the Hungarian Rebellion of 1849 and his *Eisenbahn-Dampf-Gallop* (Steam Railway Galop) was quoted by Heinrich Saro (q.v.) in his tone poem on the Franco-German War.

Andreas Leonhardt (1800-1866)

Like many great musicians, Leonhardt was from what is now the Czech Republic. He was born at Asch in the Egerland and enlisted as a bandsman in the 2nd (Emperor Alexander of Russia) Regiment in 1818. In 1823 his regiment moved to Naples, where Leonhardt, now the *Kapellmeister*, studied at the Conservatoire. He left the army in 1827 and studied in Prague under Wenzel Tomaschek, who later taught Smetana and Dvorak. In 1830, Leonhardt rejoined the army as *Kapellmeister* of the 27th (Luxem) Regiment, serving in Northern Italy and finally settling in Graz. He became Director of the Styrian Music Society in 1841 and his achievements in composing, teaching and conducting were widely acclaimed. (In an article on the Empire's military bands, written in 1846, Josef Sawerthal (q.v.) refers to "our renowned Andreas Leonhardt"). In 1850, he was summoned to Vienna and the newly-created post of *Armeekapellmeister* and this period of his life is described in Chapter Two.

Leonhardt's best known marches are the *Alexander-Cesarewitsch*, *Prinz Eugen* and *Kronprinz Rudolf* marches, though his *Retraite und Zapfenstreich*, composed for the Olmütz tattoo of 1853 is also available (2007) on CD. A recording devoted to his compositions is long overdue.

Andreas Leonhardt (1800-1866), the organiser of Austria's military music and its only *Armeekapellmeister*.

Albert Lorenz (1816- ?)

Lorenz was that rarity, a Saxon in the Prussian Army. Born in Rosswein an der Mulde, 40 km west of Dresden, the son of a weaver, he joined the 2nd Guard Lancers as a trumpeter in 1837, becoming Trumpet Major in 1850. His first success, in 1843, was a cavalry trot based on themes from the ballet *Giselle*, which became an Army March almost immediately and is still played, but it was Bote & Bock's prize competitions that brought him his greatest fame. Between 1852 and 1861, he gained seven prizes, making him the most successful participant. In 1860, three were added to the collection:

AM III 58 *Parademarsch in B Flat*, Op.164 (3rd Prize, 1858)

AM III 59 *Kavalleriemarsch in E Flat*, Op. 170 (2nd Prize, 1859)

AM III 60 *Parademarsch in A Flat*, Op. 164 (3rd Prize, 1857)

These were all popular: in 1914, fifteen cavalry regiments were using a Lorenz composition as their regimental "Walk Past". In addition, another prize winner, *Zieten aus dem Busch*, a tribute to Frederick the Great's cavalry general, was recorded by the Trumpet Corps of a Saxon Artillery regiment before the First World War, which suggests it was still in the repertoire.

Albert Lorenz retired in 1860 and seems to have vanished from history, dying some time after 1877.

Gottfried Christian Meinberg (1816-1894)

Meinberg succeeded his brother Johann Georg as *Stabshoboist* of the 2nd Foot Guards in 1849 and brought it to a high standard. (When Wieprecht chose two bands to represent Prussia at the Paris Exhibition of 1867, it was no surprise that one of them was Meinberg's.) His best known composition is his march on themes from Friedrich Flotow's opera *Grossfürstin Sophia Caterina*, which gained 2nd Prize in Bote & Bock's 1852 competition and became an Army march in the following year. In 1873 he was succeeded by his son Georg Friedrich, who served until 1895 – so the band of the 2nd Foot Guards was led by a Meinberg for fifty-one years!

August-Heinrich Neithardt (1793-1861)

Born in Schleiz in Thuringia, Neithardt grew up among the chaos of the Napoleonic Wars. In 1813, he volunteered as a horn player in the Guard *Jäger* Battalion and he became the first *Stabshornist* of the Guard Schützen Battalion in 1816. He took over from Wilhelm Nolte as *Stabshoboist* of the 33-strong band of the Kaiser Franz Grenadier Regiment and was soon a major figure in Berlin's musical life. (It was Neidhardt who introduced Wilhelm Wieprecht to military music.)

There are fourteen compositions or arrangements by Neithardt in the Army March Collection, including two based on melodies from the Swiss and Styrian Alps and one based on the *Emirs' Chorus* from Meyerbeer's *The Crusaders*. He also produced piano arrangements of famous marches, a concerto for two horns and chamber music for the same instrument. His most popular work was a setting of Bernard Thiersch's patriotic poem *Ich bin ein Preusse*, which became a second national anthem.

Neithardt's resignation in 1840 is often described as a reaction to Wieprecht's appointment as Inspector of Music, but as this had occurred two years before, this seems unlikely. He devoted himself to choral music, organising choral societies and becoming conductor of the Berlin Cathedral Choir in 1845. In 1853, he was granted honorary membership of the Royal Swedish Academy of Music – an honour later granted to Wieprecht and Leonhardt. His funeral procession was attended by the two bands he had led – a tribute to a talented and popular man.

Carl Neumann (1822 – ?)

Neumann, a Berliner, became *Stabswaldhornist* of the Guard Schutzen Battalion in 1848 and in the same year, his march based on the Austrian soldiers' song *Prinz Eugen* became an Army march. It is rarely heard today, being eclipsed by Andreas Leonhardt's version and a twentieth-century version by Josef Schifferl, but Neumann had better luck with his march on themes from Flotow's opera *Indra*, which became an Army march in 1853. A year later, he was ordered to arrange the *Pepita-Marsch*, composed around 1820 by Friedrich Pfeifke, bandmaster of the Swedish Varmland Regiment. Both these marches are still played today. In 1859, Neumann transferred to the 7th *Jäger* Battalion in Dusseldorf.

Johann Gottfried Piefke (1815–1884)

The most famous Prussian bandmaster of the period was born in Schwerin an der Warthe (now in Poland), the son of an organist, who taught him to play several instruments. He joined the 8th (*Leib*) Infantry Regiment in Frankfurt an der Oder on May 1st, 1835. In September, 1838, he began a course at Berlin's High School for Music, where he distinguished himself by his musical talent,

Johann Gottfried Piefke (1815-1884), late
in his career. Note his ornate baton.

his self-confidence and several affairs, including one with Countess Elisabeth Trachtenberg that earned him the displeasure of Queen Elisabeth of Prussia.

Piefke returned to Frankfurt as the 8th Regiment's *Stabshoboist* in June 1843. On May 24th, 1844, he gave his first "garden concert", which included an arrangement of Beethoven's *Pathetique* Sonata; his *Pochhammer-Marsch*, dedicated to his divisional commander, became an Army March in 1846. His "Berlin years" have been covered in a previous chapter, but it is worth pointing out that the 8th Regiment's band did not follow the regulation instrumentation. In 1858, it consisted of:

2 Flutes 1 A Flat Clarinet 2 E Flat Clarinets 6 Clarinets
2 Oboes 2 Bassoons 6 Trumpets 2 Flugelhorns 4 Horns
3 Euphoniums 2 Tenor Trombones 2 Bass Trombones Percussion

This departure from the rules – paraded under Wieprecht's eyes – does not appear to have harmed Piefke's career. He became a Royal Director of Music on July 23rd, 1859 and Director of Music for the whole III Army Corps – the only man to ever hold this post – on March 23rd, 1865.

After the campaigns of 1864 and 1866, *"Kapellmeister Piefke vom Leib Regiment"* was one of the best-known men in the Prussian Army. He accompanied his regiment to the Franco-German War, but fell ill during the siege of Metz and had to return to Frankfurt. When the regiment returned to their garrison, they were played in with a new march – *Preussens Gloria*.

Piefke regularly presented arrangements of classical music in his concerts, but he made no secret of his devotion to Wagner. The composer himself praised his work and when the Bayreuth Festival Theatre opened in 1876 with the premiere of the complete "Ring Cycle", Piefke was sent an invitation. Wagner's music was an article of faith to him, as was proved on one occasion after his men had performed the overture to "The Mastersingers". A gentleman approached him, hand outstretched and congratulated him on the performance, but added "although I'd far sooner hear a nice polka by Faust than that thing". Piefke, according to witnesses, seemed to grow several inches; grasping the hilt of his sword, he told the man that small children always preferred a cheap coloured picture to an Old Master drawing and some people's musical taste was no better! Then he turned on his heel and strode off. Piefke died, still serving with the 8th, on January 25th, 1884; his funeral was attended by four generals and hundreds of the citizens of Frankfurt. His grave in the Old Cemetery has been lost, but his musical legacy remains.

Piefke is reputed to have composed around sixty marches, of which twenty-five have survived. Besides the marches cited here and in Chapter 4, these include: A M II 185 *Düppler-Sturmmarsch*, A M II 186 *Düppler-Schanzen-Sturmmarsch*, A M II 189 *Siegesmarsch*, A M II 190 *Der Alsenströmer* A M II 191 *Der Lymfjordströmer* and the *Herwath-Marsch*.

These all date from the period of the Danish War. The 1866 campaign produced A M II 195 *Der Koniggrätzer* and the *Gitschiner-Marsch*, while the *Spicherer Siegesmarsch*, *Siegesmarsch von Metz*, *Neuer Pariser-Einzugsmarsch* and *Kaiser-Wilhelm-Siegesmarsch* originated in the war with France. Other compositions include the marches *Alexandrine*, *Im Hochland* and *Erinnerungen an Weimar*.

Rudolf Piefke (1835–1900)

Rudolf Piefke was born on June 3rd 1835, a month after his brother Gottfried joined the army. He volunteered as a bandsman with the 8th on October 1st, 1852 and on October 9th, 1860, he became *Stabshoboist* of the newly-formed 48th Regiment, (brigaded with the 8th) in Küstrin.

Rudolph's compositions are overshadowed by his brother's; he mainly composed dance music, but in 1866 he produced the march *Kriegers Abschied* (The Warrior's Farewell).

Johann Gottfried Rode (1797–1857)

A child prodigy who played the clarinet, violin, flute and trumpet, Rode later mastered the "Inventions-Waldhorn", a form of valved French horn. This led to a personal invitation from Major Neumann, the Commanding Officer of the Guard *Jäger* Battalion, to join his unit as the principal horn player. In 1827, he succeeded Heinrich Schumann as *Stabswaldhornist* and on May 1st, 1835, he became a Royal Music Director. His feud with Wilhelm Wieprecht over the composition of *Jäger* bands was carried on after his death by his son Theodor and Wieprecht left the *Jägers'* all-brass instrumentation alone. (It remained in use until World War II.)

Rode, who was still serving when he died, composed over three thousand works, but the only one to remain in the repertoire is his march *Der Jäger aus Kurpfalz*, which uses the old song in the trio. Curiously, this did not become an Army March until 1913!

Heinrich Saro (1827-1891), bandmaster of the 'Franzers' from 1859 to 1887 and Wieprecht's *de facto* successor as Inspector of Army Music.

Heinrich Saro (1827 – 1891)

Saro enlisted in the band of the Guard Schützen Battalion in 1846 and in 1853, his arrangements of two cavalry marches by Julius Möllendorf' were added to the official collection. (*Parademarsch Nr. 1* is still widely played and can often be heard – as "Möllendorf's Parade March" – during the Queen's Birthday Parade.) On May 1st, 1856 he became *Stabshoboist* of the 11th Infantry in Breslau, with Friedrich Wilhelm, the future Crown Prince, as his commanding officer. The same year, he gained 3rd Prize in Bote & Bock's competition with his *Prinz-Friedrich-Wilhelm-Marsch*.

1859 was an important year for Saro; he won 1st Prize in that year's competition with his *Defiliermarsch* and, on Prince Friedrich Wilhelm's recommendation, succeeded Wilhelm Christoph as *Stabshoboist* of the Kaiser Franz Grenadiers on May 1st. He would hold this post until his retirement. In 1867, his band and that of the 2nd Foot Guards were combined by Wieprecht into an ensemble that gained 1st prize at the Paris International Exhibition. (While he was in Paris, he arranged Olivier Metra's waltz *Les Roses* as a march and performed it before Napoleon III.) His service in the Franco-German War gained him the Iron Cross 2nd Class and in 1872, he took his band to Boston for a four week tour. Saro helped organise a school for military bandmasters in Berlin and wrote what became the standard textbook for military band instrumentation, *Instrumentalslehre für Militärmusik*. His other compositions included a "Bombardonmarsch" on themes from Heinrich Bruell's opera "The Golden Cross" and a tone poem on the Franco-German War, *Kriegserrinerungenvon 1870–1871*. After Wieprecht's death in 1872, Saro was *de facto* Inspector of Army Music until his retirement on health grounds in 1887.

Josef Sawerthal (1819–1893)

Born in Leitmeritz (Litomerice) in Bohemia, Sawerthal served with the 6th Cuirassiers, then became *Kapellmeister* of the 53rd Infantry in 1843. In 1850, he transferred to the Navy where he came into contact with Archduke Maximillian and when Maximillian left Trieste for Mexico on the frigate *Novara*, Sawerthal accompanied him as head of the Imperial Mexican Music Service. (His march *IMS Novara* was played as the frigate left port.) After the collapse of the Mexican Empire, Sawerthal returned to Europe, but not to Austria – he took up a post in Britain as civilian bandmaster of the 2nd Battalion, 4th (King's Own) Regiment in 1868. In 1871, he transferred to the Royal Engineers at Chatham, where he built up a band that doubled as a symphony orchestra. However, his *Royal Engineers Quick March*, intended to replace the Corps' march *Wings*, met with widespread disapproval and the score remained in the archives of the British Library until it was recorded in 2006. Sawerthal retired on health grounds in 1889 and died in Leitmeritz four years later.

Friedrich Wilhelm Voigt (1833–1894)

Voigt was born in Coblenz, the son of *Stabshoboist* Christian Voigt of the 30th Infantry. He studied in Leipzig and Berlin, where his "graduation exercise", a choral symphony based on Luther's *Ein feste Burg* won him the Silver Medal of the Royal Academy of Arts and Sciences. In 1857, when he was in the orchestra of the Royal Opera, Wilhelm Wieprecht recommended that he succeed Carl Engelhardt as *Stabshoboist* of the 1st Foot Guards in Potsdam and the authorities agreed, on condition that Voigt was enlisted and given (very) basic training. No one wanted a repetition of the problems Wieprecht's appointment had caused.

Voigt was responsible for the musical side of much court and military ceremonial and was a popular figure with the royal family, especially with King Wilhelm, with whom he shared a birthday. It became traditional for the 1st Foot Guards' birthday serenade to conclude with king and conductor exchanging greetings! When Voigt's seventh child, Wilhelm Ludwig Emil was christened in 1872, the King was one of his godfathers. In 1887, Voigt took up the post of Inspector of Army Music; he retired in 1890 and moved to Bernburg, where he died four years later. His funeral in Potsdam was attended by the *Leib* (Sovereign's) Company of the 1st Guards and he was borne to the grave to the sound of the funeral march he had composed for the burial of Friedrich Wilhelm IV in 1861.

Voigt produced a large number of marches, including the *Angriffs-Kolonnen-Marsch, deutsche Feldherren, Kaiser-Friedrich-Fanfare, Der 30. Januar, 1866, Die Deutsche Kaisergarde, Stoltzenfels-Marsch, Drei-Kaiser-Marsch, Krakowiak Aus Oesterreich* (based on the dance performed by the men of the King of Prussia's Regiment in Berlin November 1864) and *Salus Caesari Nostro Gullielmo*, which commemorates the proclamation of Wilhelm I as German Emperor and includes "See the Conquering Hero Comes" from Handel's *Judas Maccabeus* in the trio. He also made many arrangements of classical works.

Wilhelm Wieprecht (1802–1872)

Wieprecht was born in Aschersleben, the son of a musician and trained both as a brass player and as a violinist as his father believed it would give him more opportunities. In 1820, he joined the Gewandhaus Orchestra in Leipzig and moved to Berlin four years later, joining the Royal Opera orchestra under Gasparo Spontini on May 2nd. Shortly afterwards, he discovered what was to be his career. After his success organising the Trumpet Corps of the Guard Dragoons, he was asked to train the trumpeters of the Guard Hussars in Potsdam and in 1835, he was sent to the 2nd Cavalry Brigade in Danzig. During this period, he was busy composing and building up a network of contacts, notably with the royal family. All this work bore fruit when he was appointed Inspector of Music for the Guard and Grenadier Corps on February 2nd, 1838. His achievements are described in Chapter 1, but it is worth mentioning that his first "monster concert" occurred when Tsar Nicholas I visited Berlin the same year. Sixteen infantry and sixteen cavalry bands – a total of 1,086 musicians and 105 drummers – paraded in the square in front of the Royal Palace under Wieprecht's baton. In 1847, he was asked to reorganise Turkey's military bands and five years later a similar request arrived from Guatemala. This shows that Wieprecht had a worldwide reputation.

Perhaps Wieprecht's greatest triumph came in July 1867. The Paris International Exhibition included a military music competition and Wieprecht conducted the combined bands of the 2nd Foot Guards and the Kaiser Franz Guard Grenadiers. The Prussians gained the highest score, but the judges, aware of the politics involved, awarded three First Prizes, with the others going to the Austrian 76th Regiment and the Garde de Paris (the forerunners of today's Garde Republicaine). On his return to Berlin, Wieprecht presented the Gold Medal to the King, but was told, "No, my dear Wieprecht, you have earned the medal, not me." After a prolonged period of ill-health, Wieprecht died in Berlin on August 4th, 1872.

Wilhelm Wieprecht with the combined bands of the 2nd Foot Guards and Emperor Francis Guard Grenadiers, photographed at the Paris Exhibition of 1867, where he won First Prize. He is flanked by the two bandmasters, Meinberg (l.) and Saro.

An advertisement from 1866 for one of
Wieprecht's 'Monster Concerts', part of a
fundraising concert for soldiers' families.

Wieprecht's compositions are rarely played today and his arrangements
have been superseded by those of Grawert, Hackenberger and Diesenroth, but
a selection of both is currently (2007) available on CD (see "Recommended
Recordings"). This includes two of his *Sechs Märsche fur Kavallerie-Musik* of
1825, the *Cavallerie-Marsch* composed for the Guard Dragoons in 1829, a march
composed for King Friedrich Wilhelm IV's entry into Berlin on September
21st 1840 and the *Viktoria-Marsch*, which will be of interest to British readers.
Composed (as the *Prinzess-Royal-Viktoria-Marsch*) to celebrate the entry of Queen
Victoria's eldest daughter into Berlin on February 8th 1858, after her marriage
to the future Crown Prince, it features "Rule Britannia" in the trio. (When the
Princess became Colonel-in-Chief of the 2nd Hussars, the regiment adopted the
march as their regimental "Walk Past", discarding the beautiful march Carl Maria
von Weber had composed for them in 1822.) Wieprecht's other cavalry marches
include two on themes from operas (Johann Reichardt's *Brennus* and Meyerbeer's
Ein Feldlager in Schlesien) two celebrating the centenaries of the Garde du Corps
and the 2nd Hussars and one dedicated to the Berlin Sharpshooters' Guild. All
these became Army Marches, as did his arrangements of marches by Ernest von
Danckelmann, Johann Schubert and Gaetano Donizetti's march honouring
Sultan Mahmud II, while in 1837, eight "signals" (pre-1806 regimental marches
which could be used as fanfares or cavalry "trots") were added. (The first, the old
march of the Garde du Corps, was still in use in 1939 as the *Standarten-Fanfare*,
while the march of the *Gens d'Armes* Regiment was passed on to Wieprecht
by Friedrich Wilhelm III, who sang it for him.) Wieprecht's compositions
for infantry band include *Links-Rechts*, *Schon Heil!* and a march based on the
Musketeers' Dance from Peter Hertel's ballet *Satanella*; he also arranged a group

of eighteenth century marches as *Prasentiermärsche*. These were so popular that more "authentic" versions discovered in the 1890s failed to supplant them.

With his background, it was natural for Wieprecht to see the military band as a "wind orchestra", interpreting classical works. His arrangement of Berlioz's *Francs Juges* overture – and the composer's reaction – was described in Chapter 1 and this was only one arrangement among hundreds. At the Paris Exhibition, each band played a test piece (the overture to Weber's *Oberon*) and a piece of their own choosing; Wieprecht composed a fantasy on themes from Meyerbeer's *Le Prophete* and it was perhaps fitting that this piece gained him his greatest honour.

The contribution of this bespectacled, unsoldierly man to Prussian military music cannot be overstated. He, more than anyone else, created the "modern" Prussian military band and his introduction of the new valved instruments produced the "sound" we take for granted. His establishment of a unified system of scoring was of lasting value and he helped Prussian bands to gain a worldwide reputation. His triumph at the Paris Exhibition only confirmed his standing as the most important Prussian musical personality of the period.

It is pleasant to record that Wieprecht, despite his many honours, remained a simple, friendly man, popular with his musicians and concerned for their welfare. He established relief funds for musicians' widows and orphans and was the prime mover behind the pension fund for bandmasters established by the Prussian War Ministry in 1859.

Emil Winter (? – c.1870)

Winter was *Stabshoboist* of the 5th Infantry (later Grenadiers) in Danzig between 1844 and 1866. He was the second most successful competitor in Bote & Bock's competitions, with his *Kolonnen-Marsch* (3rd Prize, 1853), *Elisabeth-Marsch* (2nd Prize, 1854), *Friedrich-Wilhelm-Marsch* (finalist, 1855) and *Manövrier-Marsch* (2nd Prize, 1856). The first and last of these became Army Marches in 1860. Winter was awarded the General Military Decoration in 1855.

Bibliography

Many of the sources cited here are out of print and foreign language material is extremely difficult to obtain through the public library interloan system. Readers are recommended to consult the publisher's website (www.helion.co.uk) or that of Berliner Zinnfiguren (www.zinnfigur.de). Both feature a wide selection of new and out of print material and both firms issue regular catalogues. The specialist English-language society for this period is the Continental Wars Society, who issue a regular journal, *The Foreign Correspondent*. Contact Ralph Weaver at 37, Yeading Avenue, Rayners Lane, Harrow, Middlesex HA2 9RL. Anyone seriously interested in military music should contact the International Military Music Society (www.int-militarymusicsoc.org). Their journal, *Band International*, appears three times a year and branches have their own newsletter. Of the authors cited below, I would particularly recommend Joachim Toeche-Mittler and Eugen Brixel, without whom this book could never have been written and Gordon Craig, who first introduced me to this campaign, nearly forty years ago.

Bader, Werner *Pionier Klinke* (Berlin: Westkreuz, 1992)

Benedek, Ludwig von *Tactical and general instructions for the Imperial Royal Northern Army* (Tonbridge: Pallas Armata, 1996)

Brixel, Eugen et. al *Das ist Oesterreichs Militärmusik* (Graz: Kaleidoscop, 1982)

Busch, Heinz *Vom Armee Marsch zum Grossen Zapfenstreich* (Bonn: Kurier, 2005)

Campaign of 1866 in Germany, compiled by the Department of Military History of the Prussian Staff (HMSO: 1872. Reprinted Nashville: Battery Press, 1991)

Craig, Gordon *The Battle of Königgrätz* (London: Weidenfeld & Nicolson, 1965)

Embree, Michael *Bismarck's First War: The Campaign of Schleswig and Jutland 1864* (Solihull: Helion, 2006)

Fontane, Theodor *Der Deutsche Krieg von 1866 Band I* (Berlin: Decker, 1870)

Hermann, Gustav "Die Armee-Musik-Inspizienten" in *Deutsches SoldatenJahrbuch* 1970 (Munich: Schild, 1969)

Hönig, Fritz *The Tactics of the Future* (1899: reprinted Tonbridge: Pallas Armata, 1994)

Hozier, Henry M *The Seven Weeks War* (1867: reprinted Minneapolis: Absinthe, 1991)

Muller, Reinhold *Spielmann-Trompeter-Hoboist* (Berlin: Militärverlag der DDR, 1988)

Pavlovic, Darko *The Austrian Army, 1836-1866 2 Volumes* (Reading: Osprey, 1999)

Pietsch, Paul *Formations-und Uniformierungsgeschichte des Preussichen Heeres 1808 bis 1914 2 Volumes* (Hamburg: Schulz, 1963, 1966)

Preil, Arndt *Oesterreichs Schlachtfelder 4: Trautenau, Nachod Skalitz, Koniggrätz* (Graz: Weishaupt, 1997)

Rieben, F von *Geschichte des königlich preussichen Kaiser-Franz-Garde-Grenadier Regiment Nr.2 2 Volumes* (Berlin: Parey, 1914)

Spielhagen, Paul & Schlegel "Die Kapellmeister des preussichen Gardekorps _____" *Zeitschrift für Heereskunde* 1969–1971

Toeche-Mittler, Joachim *Armeemärsche 3 Volumes* (Neckargemund: Vowinckel, 1971, 1975)

Vajda, Stefan *Mir san von k.u.k – die küriose Geschichte des Oesterreichischen Militärmusiks* (Vienna: Überreuter, 1975)

Voigt, Gunther *Deutschlands Heere bis 1918 Band 1* (Osnabruck: Biblio: 1980)

Wawro, Geoffrey *The Austro-Prussian War* (Cambridge: CUP, 1996)

Recommended Recordings

Many of the classic marches of the period such as Leonhardt's *Alexandermarsch* or Faust's *Defiliermarsch* are widely available on CD, but bands and record companies show little imagination in their choice of material and stick to the old favourites. The best source for German and Austrian military CDs is Berliner Zinnfiguren, 88 Knesebeckstrasse, Berlin-Charlottenberg 10623 (www.zinnfigur.de). In the UK, Discurio, Unit 3, Faraday Way, St. Mary Cray, Kent BR5 3QW (www.tillystips.com/dis) stock German and Austrian recordings, including second hand LPs. Both suppliers can be recommended unreservedly.

Nearly half the Prussian Army March Collection is covered by two sets of recordings. In 1959, Philips released the five volumes of *Deutsche Armeemärsche*, with Oberst-Leutnant Wilhelm Stephan conducting the Stabsmusikkorps der Bundeswehr. Its eighty tracks cover music from the mid-seventeenth to the mid-twentieth century and include many of the classics as well as rarities such as Gung'l's *Kriegers Lust*. The set was issued on a bargain CD label in the 1990s, but is currently (2007) unavailable: it should be snapped up when it reappears. In the early 1970s, an outstanding series of LPs appeared on the Telefunken label, with Heeresmusikkorps 5 performing under the baton of Oberstleutnant Heinrich Schlüter, with some tracks conducted by Oberst Johannes Schade, the Bundeswehr's Inspector of Music at the time. Nine of these LPs have now appeared on a 5-CD set, *Deutsche Heeresmärsche* (Braun BCD 278/1-5). They include some unfamiliar marches from the Prussian collection, as well as some from other German states. A bonus is a selection of Wilhelm Wieprecht's compositions and arrangements. This is one of the most important issues of recent years and no one who is seriously interested in military music should miss it.

The only other composer of this period to have recordings dedicated to his work is Gottfried Piefke. *Preussiche Armeemärsche – Gottfried Piefke* (Studio Classique SC 100 314) features thirteen of his marches played by the Stabsmusikkorps Berlin under Oberstleutnant Volker Wörrlein. This is a good selection, but the producers decided to fill the second half of the CD with another recording of the *Grosser Zapfenstreich* ceremony. A wider selection of marches and dances by Gottfried and his brother is contained in *Die Piefkes kommen – Märsche und Tänze von Gottfried und Rudolf Piefke* (Antenne CD 9503 POFO) played by the Polizeiorchester Frankfurt am Oder conducted by Jurgen Bludowsky, with twenty-two tracks covering much unfamiliar material. Since the CD's release in 1995, the band has been merged into the Landespolizeiorchester Brandenburg and this recording is only available from their supporters group (www.internetwache-brandenburg.de/alias/lapob). The Brandenburg police have also produced two volumes of *Brillante Märsche* (AMOS 5963& 6009) which are among the outstanding recordings of recent years.

For the Austrians, the starting point must be the Militärmusik Salzburg's seven discs of *Historische Regimentsmärsche der k.u.k Armee* (Koch 321 170; 321 696; 324 780; 323 646; 323 849; 324 324 & 324 901). These cover the marches of all 102 Infantry regiments in 1914, but, as I have pointed out above, only a selection of them are marches used in 1866. More historical music can be heard on *40 Jahre Militärmusik Salzburg 1956–1996* (Koch 323 679) and *Soldatisches Musik einst und Jetzt* by the Militärmusik Kärnten under Sigmund Seidl (Koch 322112). The latter contains the only recording of Leonhardt's *Retraite und Zapfenstreich zu Olmütz*. Finally, a large number of archive recordings have been issued by Jubal Musik of Berlin (www.jubal.de). The series began with six CDs of recordings from the 1950s by the Berlin Schutzenpolizei under the legendary Heinz Winkel, which includes many of the classic marches. (*Deutsche Marschmusik mit Heinz Winkel*: Jubal 001101/ 020201/ 030626/031001/040301/041001). Jubal have now begun a series of CDs of recordings from before the First World War and the inter-war period and the first, *Preussische Marschmusik* (Jubal 050601) features a wide selection of infantry and cavalry bands (including a performance by the 43rd Infantry featuring one of their "drum dogs"). This has now been followed by CDs of Bavarian and Saxon music. All these recordings give a good idea of the Prussian and Austrian repertoire of the time and we can only hope that more of this material will become available.

Related titles published by Helion & Company

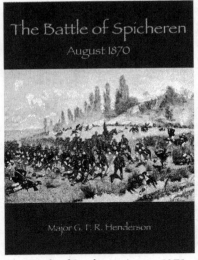

The Battle of Spicheren August 1870
Major G.F.R. Henderson
256pp   Paperback
ISBN 978 1 874622 44 4

A Reply to the Prussian Campaign of 1866, A Tactical Retrospect
Colonel P.L.E.A.H. Bronsart
von Schellendorf
68pp   Paperback
ISBN 978 1 906033 04 0

Related titles

The Prussian Campaign of 1866
Capt. Theodor May 978 1 874622 14

The Strategy of the Seven Weeks' War 1866
Major A.D. Gillespie-Addison 978 1 874622 55

The Bohemian Battlefields of 1866
Lieutenant J.H.M. Cornwall 978 1 874622 98

The Battle of Koniggratz
Col. Walker 978 1874622 09

HELION & COMPANY
26 Willow Road, Solihull, West Midlands B91 1UE, England
Telephone 0121 705 3393   Fax 0121 711 4075
Website: http://www.helion.co.uk